MW01634121

"CRAZY" MIGHT BE A BLESSING IN DISGUISE!

by
Kris Castro, P.C.C.
Shift Inc.™

www.BeginToShift.com/Crazy-Adventure-Book

Copyright © 2019
Kris Castro, P.C.C.
www.BeginToShift.com/Crazy-Adventure-Book
All Rights Reserved

"CRAZY" MIGHT BE A BLESSING IN DISGUISE!

No part of this book may be reproduced or transmitted in any form or by any means, electronic or mechanical, including photocopying, recording, or by any information storage and retrieval system, without permission in writing from the publisher. Permission to quote brief excerpts for review is granted without further permission when accompanied by publication data.

Disclaimer: This book contains advice and information. The publisher and author disclaim liability for any psychological or medical outcomes that may occur as a result of any of the suggestions in this book.

Published by Shift Inc.™ (www.BeginToShift.com)
ISBN 978-0-9849855-6-2 (paperback)

For more information email Kris@BeginToShift.com or call 404-551-3601.

Table of Contents

DEDICATION

So many people made this Adventure possible by listening to the Lord's prompting to provide a place for me to stay, financial gifts to cover gas and expenses, and offering too many meals to count.

I want to especially thank my Mom and Dad for being supportive of my decision to pack everything up and follow the Lord on this "Crazy" Adventure! I love you both very much and truly honor your position as my earthly parents in addition to having a Heavenly Daddy who is always there when I need Him.

Specific people I would like to recognize who significantly impacted my life for a variety of reasons are as follows: Christina Hice, Meg Crowley, Patti Adair, Rick Meekins, Yodit Beshah, Brenda Earley, Barbara Gibb, Tami Sherry, Laura Kent, my CR Step-Sisters, Laure Hoffman, Kimberlee Scott, the Council of Leaders group, and Patty Sadallah.

Thanks also to all the CR Leaders across the U.S. who coordinated my visit to each of your groups and the people who opened their homes to me each night.

May the Lord bless each of you richly and return what you gave me 7-fold as a sign of His honor towards you for taking care of me however He led you to do so.

Thanks again, everyone! :) ~Kris

Introduction

  As I put down my checkbook in frustration, I looked upward and sarcastically said to the Lord, "If you're not going to provide enough money for rent next month I may as well put all my stuff in storage, pack up my car, and travel across the U.S. catching up with people I haven't seen in a while." After a few seconds of silence, I sighed deeply, put my checkbook away, and went on with my day.

  The following week during a visit with friends, I shared what I said to the Lord. Then suddenly, without even a glimmer of thought, out of my mouth came the words, "It would certainly be a G-d[1] Adventure where I can be His hands and feet for people He places in my path, and I can offer to give my Celebrate Recovery Testimony in CR locations across the USA along my journey."

  The moment I finished that sentence I knew my flippant comment a week earlier had suddenly become a divine invitation to deepen my faith and my intimacy with the Lord by going on a journey similar to Abraham: "By faith, Abraham, when called to go to a place he would later receive as his inheritance, obeyed and went, even though he did not know where he was going" (Hebrews 11:8 / ESV).

  In my heart I suspected the Lord prompted that unintended comment, but in reality it made no sense so I wrestled with it for a few days. After all, I wasn't excited about giving up the room I was renting to essentially live out of my car and "couch surf" for an unspecified amount of time until the Lord turned around my financial situation.

---

[1] *Why do I spell G_d with an underline instead of an "o"?* I adopted that tradition after I joined a Messianic Jewish / Gentile Congregation. It shows a deep sign of respect for our Lord's name. To learn more, check out this resource: Rabbinical Halakhah – Writing the Hebrew Names of God at http://www.hebrew4christians.com/Names_of_G-d/About_Writing/about_writing.html

Not to mention, how would I pay the bills which have to be paid no matter what my life looks like at any given moment? I generate some income as a contractor for a consultant I work with a few hours a month, but it's certainly not enough to cover all my expenses. Realistically, it would be far more logical to put my company on hold and get a part-time job until things turned around.

The G-d Adventure invitation seemed like a crazy idea in my situation.....and yet the more I prayed over the next few days, the more I continually sensed the Lord telling me that this "crazy" adventure would lay the foundation for all the blessings He planned on giving me in the next season of my life.

I would like to say when I sensed what He wanted that I automatically responded, "Yes, Lord, your will be done!" -- but I didn't. Instead I said, "Really? Are you sure? Can I have some confirmation before I totally uproot my life again for the 4th time in two years?"

Despite that uncertainty, the Lord knows my heart's desire is to be totally surrendered to Him. Within a week He lovingly provided three confirmations (all in one day) from various newsletters, devotions, and a women's conference I watched online. The first confirmation made me laugh out loud: In Todd White's newsletter, the first sentence was: "...Summertime is a perfect time to go on <u>God adventures</u> with your family and friends...." (underline is my emphasis).

How much more direct does the Lord have to be with me? Much more, it seems, because even after I received those three confirmations, I still resisted and asked for one more (remember Gideon, anyone??). I'm sure the Lord was humorously smiling at my need for more certainty. He honored me yet again by providing another newsletter confirmation from a different organization which stated: "Take time and days, even seasons, to have days off and to go on a sabbatical trip with the Lord."

It was pointless to avoid the truth any longer. I knew the Lord was giving me a choice to go on the Adventure with Him rather than try to fix my financial situation my way.

The Lord often used the financial area of my life to get my attention for any one of the following reasons: a) to re-direct me, b) to heal something inside of me, or c) to stop me long enough to deal with something before I can advance to whatever he has for me next. Whatever His reason, it's always to set me up for something better.

Over the last year I had gone through an extensive healing process (that's how I got into Celebrate Recovery[2] / CR) and also worked through several things which needed to be dealt with. Therefore, it seems this trip is a re-direct to develop additional skills and spiritual gifts before the Lord reveals whatever He has planned for the next season of my life. His way is always much better than my way, so I let my landlord know what I was up to and began to prepare to head out in a few weeks.

Since the Lord personally invited me on this Adventure with Him, I am excited about all the amazing things that are bound to happen and I am also somewhat apprehensive about the uncertainty of it all. Objectively I know the Lord is Jehovah Jireh, my Provider, and He will go before me to prepare my way (Deuteronomy 31:8). Therefore, I am choosing faith and will partner with the spirit of joy as I prepare to leave, commanding anxiety, worry and fear to BE GONE, in the name of Yeshua (Jesus' Hebrew name).

****

As I reflect on that providential day in June, I am still in awe of everything that has occurred over the past seven months. I left on the Adventure as a woman on fire for the Lord, and returned with more intensity, an even deeper level of faith, and a fuller assurance that the Lord loves to show up and show off when we honor Him through our obedience.

This book is a combination of the blog entries I shared throughout my Adventure along with deeper dives into

---

[2] If you are interested in learning more about Celebrate Recovery, here is the website: www.CelebrateRecovery.com.

topics the Lord laid on my heart as I was writing the book. Some of the blog entries are videos, and a link has been provided in the book for you to view them.

My suggestion is to not skip ahead as you read through the book or watch all the videos at once. The faith journey and the lessons I learned during the Adventure happened in the order the Lord arranged on purpose. Like any great story, I encourage you to read this book as it occurred and watch how the Lord speaks to you from chapter to chapter.

Before you begin, take a moment to ask the Lord to highlight the information that is important for your life right now because He knows what you need to know as you move into the next season of your life.

I had no idea when I left Atlanta that my "Crazy" Adventure would truly become a blessing in disguise!

May this book be a blessing to you as well, and may my story be a catalyst for you to take the first step towards your own Adventure with the Lord!

~ Kris Castro

Chapter 1 - Broken Becomes Beautiful In Time

"Hi! My name is Kris and I am in recovery for Codependency...."

That is my opening sentence when I share my testimony at a Celebrate Recovery (CR) group. Little did I know the first few times I shared it in Georgia that the Lord was going to ask me to deliver it to CR groups across the country.

Like most good stories, there is always a back story explaining the events and decisions which caused someone to arrive at a certain point in life. To put my Adventure in context, here is part of my back story to show how I got involved in Celebrate Recovery:

Several years ago, I began experiencing an ongoing and extremely difficult challenge with one of the relationships in my life. As I was praying through that situation, the Lord made it clear this relationship was very important to my future and asked me to continue to trust the promise He made previously that the relationship would eventually be healed.

Since the Lord asked me to trust Him, I moved forward in faith, and because He had never failed me before I continued to trust Him despite the emotional rollercoaster I was experiencing on a regular basis.

You may be wondering why I was willing to step out in faith when everything inside me just wanted to cut this person loose from my life. Let's just say it wasn't the first time the Lord asked me to trust Him with a difficult relationship. That story begins with my parents.

****

My Mom and Dad grew up in very different environments. My mother's mother used control and explosive anger when she raised my mother and her sister; and that became my mother's weapon of choice in our family. In my father's family, my grandfather had a history of alcoholism and affairs, so my grandmother left him and moved from Texas to NYC causing my father to have to become the man of the house at 12-years old, find a job to help pay the bills, and care for his two sisters.

My father's mother never re-married. There was very little arguing, and rarely outbursts of anger in their household because my grandmother wouldn't allow it. Needless to say, when my father married my mother they had no idea their dramatically different childhoods would cause an incredible amount of unavoidable conflict between them that would negatively affect each of us kids.

Growing up, I always got along with my Dad. He was the safe parent who made rational decisions and I enjoyed spending time with him. I knew my mother loved me, but because most days she acted like an angry time bomb just waiting to go off - and because I never knew when it would happen or why - I spent my childhood walking on eggshells to avoid her irrational outbursts or digging in and fighting to defend myself whenever she treated me unfairly. The older I got, the more determined I became to defend myself. And the more I stood up to my Mom, the more our relationship deteriorated.

Between the regular heated arguments that happened several times a week between Mom and Dad, and the spill-over arguments that happened between Mom and us kids, our home was pretty much filled with a constant tension of anger. Like most kids I managed to survive through it, and by my Junior Year of High School I became a very independent, confident, outspoken, and fun-loving woman who loved Jesus more than life. I always knew the Lord was with me, so I took everything life threw at me and made the best of it, trusting Him with the results.

After high school graduation I headed off to college thrilled to have 300 glorious miles between me and my mother. And then the most unexpected thing happened. Three months into my Freshman year, the Holy Spirit prompted me to reconcile with my mother. My first reaction was not exactly godly. I believe what I said to the Lord was, "YOU ARE CRAZY! I chose a college five hours from home so I WOULDN'T be near her. Now that I've finally escaped you want me to open a door for another relationship with her? SERIOUSLY G-D, what are you thinking??"

After arguing a while with G-d, I decided He probably knew best and stepped out in faith to reconcile with my mother. What I didn't know at the time is that she had already begun to attend therapy and was much more capable of having a healthy relationship with me. Our first conversation went better than I expected, and after a few years of building trust and healing our relationship, I now count my Mom as one of my greatest friends.

That was the first of many times the Lord would show me ANY relationship can be healed and restored to some degree - if not completely - by trusting in Him and His redemptive process instead of what I feel or think about a situation.

Fast forward to age 30, I got engaged, but every moment I moved closer to the wedding my anxiety about it grew exponentially until I finally postponed the wedding which unexpectedly led me into an emotional breakdown followed by intense therapy in which much of my childhood drama was brought from my subconscious to my conscious mind so I could finally deal with it.

It was the first time I heard the word "Codependency" and began to understand why my engagement and relationship had been such a disaster. I emerged from therapy radically transformed and had a much better understanding of how to love someone with healthy expectations. I also excelled at setting better boundaries which would serve me very well throughout the rest of my life.

****

You should now have enough context to comprehend why I chose to trust the Lord and willingly maintained the difficult relationship I mentioned at the beginning of this chapter.

After I made that commitment to the Lord, a lot happened over the next two years; most of which was extremely emotionally draining. I questioned G-d many times about His desire for me to hold onto that relationship and wondered if I was crazy to believe in a promise that made absolutely no sense in real life.

But G-d kept telling me to trust Him, and who was I to put my foot down and tell G-d He was crazy after spending my whole life in various experiences watching His version of "crazy" become beautiful when He got done with it. Between G-d's promise and additional signs to continue moving forward, I did, with hopeful expectation He would honor my obedience in the face of the emotional strain I was experiencing on a regular basis.

Another year went by with no positive changes and things even got worse. I couldn't fathom why the Lord was delaying His promise despite my obedience in following

His will. My extreme exhaustion in having to interact with this person and my increasing disappointment in the Lord for not fixing the situation began a time of questioning everything I ever believed about G-d, my faith, His character, and His goodness in general. I was not prepared for the crisis of faith I was experiencing during that season.

As that relationship situation got even more emotionally intense, my cries to G-d and my ocean of tears seemed to fall on deaf ears. No amount of praying, begging, quoting scripture, and reminding the Lord of His promise did any good. I was broken spiritually and emotionally and did not know how to survive any longer in the relationship G-d had asked me to maintain.

By this time my anger at the whole situation and the years G-d had ignored me started getting the best of me to the point I was having trouble managing my own anger within that relationship. I also found myself constantly furious with G-d. The more emotionally and spiritually broken I became, the less I was capable of trusting G-d to come through with His promise, which made me even less capable of responding to this person in love the way G-d continued to ask of me.

One day during a particularly volatile argument, I snapped, mentally left my body, and watched myself in slow motion push this person into a wall out of sheer rage and exhaustion from having to deal with that situation for years with no indication that the relationship was ever going to improve. As I was pulled back into my body, I heard this person say something like, "Don't touch me. I'm going to call the cops because you are going to hurt me." I stared at this person intently, and with an eerie tone of icy challenge I responded, "If I wanted to hurt you, I would've grabbed a sharp utensil from the kitchen."

The moment I uttered those words I suddenly realized what I was capable of, quickly apologized and said I shouldn't have done it, then walked rapidly away - afraid of what I might do next or what that person might do in response.

A deep well of fear raced through me as I recognized I needed help before I did something far worse. It also became clear I had completely lost my identity in Christ and my identity in what made me, me; all because of an unfulfilled promise from the Lord and years of continuous suffering as I waited for that promise to come true.

The next day I called one of my friends and shared what happened. She suggested I attend Celebrate Recovery (CR) to help me rebuild my faith and release the rage and intense hurt inside me from years of maintaining that relationship. She had been in CR for a long time and it truly changed her life; and I was willing to try anything at this point to stabilize my shaky faith and find myself again.

The first night I attended CR I instantly knew I was in the right place. From the people I met during dinner, to the program speakers, to the open share groups one thing was certain: everyone who was serious about their recovery was "owning their stuff." G-d even arranged for the Step-Study program to be open for two more weeks so I could to jump into my recovery more quickly and deeply. That 12-step program became the key to my recovery and healing, and the weekly CR meetings became my lifeline week after week back to sanity.

I promise you, nothing in Celebrate Recovery happens by accident. The ladies the Lord placed around me in the open share groups, the Sponsor He gave me, and all my Step-Study Sisters were divinely arranged. Each person became a piece of understanding in my recovery, leading me one step closer to the joy and peace I was desperately craving as I continued my journey to find myself again.

Over the next year as I progressed through the CR program, I saw so many substantial changes happen in various areas of my life. One of the most significant was during Step 8 after I wrote my amends letter to G-d for the time I doubted His goodness and truly questioned His character.

On this side of my healing and recovery journey I now understand why I lost faith in the Lord during the worst of that challenging relationship. It was because my faith was built on previous faith experiences with G-d rather than who He is regardless of those experiences.

I see now He used those silent years to move me into a new and deeply intimate relationship with Him - one where He is my Lord & King first and my Daddy second. Today I stand before Him as both a Faithful Warrior and Beloved Daughter who is diligently trusting in His unchangeable character and committed to looking at all things from spiritual eyes instead of earthly perspectives; no matter how difficult the circumstance.

Two of the most substantial lessons the Lord taught me while in the CR program are as follows:

1) *Surrendering everything, especially the timing of an un-fulfilled promise, is the key to waiting well.* Step 3 in the recovery process is what I call the "Complete Surrender" step. It was the hardest part of my journey, and also the most transformational because once I let go of all my expectations and my desired control of the outcome, peace and joy

showed up more easily. <u>I find it ironic that the more you surrender, the more freedom you receive!</u>

2) *Just because something looks dead, doesn't mean it is.* Even though that relationship is just as challenging today as it was back then, I am now more confident the promise the Lord gave me years ago is NOT dead despite my current circumstances seeming otherwise. I recognize G-d used the delay in keeping His promise to prune <u>my</u> character and give <u>me</u> opportunities to develop new spiritual gifts which never would have occurred to the depth they are occurring right now if His promise had not been delayed. Without the lessons I've learned and the deeper level of faith I've grown into through the suffering I've experienced over the last five years, I never would have been prepared to step into the higher level of leadership and Kingdom impact G-d is calling me into through my business and ministry opportunities around me.

Romans 5:3-5 has become a reality for me through that entire experience: *"But not only that, let us also boast in our troubles; because we know that trouble produces endurance, endurance produces character, and character produces hope; and this hope does not let us down, because God's love for us has already been poured out in our hearts through the Ruach HaKodesh [the Jewish word for Holy Spirit] who has been given to us"* (CJB).

Because of what I went through, I have immensely more endurance during trials than I ever did before. My character has also been deeply pruned by the Lord to get rid of what wasn't serving me well, replacing those areas with enhanced spiritual qualities. All of which has produced deeper hope and trust in the Lord.

I don't know what you are going through at this very moment, but I can assure you that the Lord sees your pain and is with you in that circumstance despite the silence you may be feeling. Sometimes His silence is purposeful because the timing isn't right or He's using the experience as a growth opportunity. Other times His silence may be occurring because you have put spiritual obstacles in His path. For example, there was a time when I had so much unforgiveness, resentment and bitterness towards the person in my story that it completely prevented the Lord from responding to my prayers (see 1 Peter 3:12).

A resource which helped me clear out some of the obstacles between myself and the Lord, and heal more of the unhealthy emotional baggage I was carrying around, is a ministry called Restoring the Foundations. As I worked with them to remove many of those self-imposed spiritual obstacles, I began to feel more at peace in my relationship with the Lord even though my situation had not yet changed.

I know it may not seem like it now, but your brokenness will become beautiful over time if you surrender it to the Lord.

Let Him guide you through your own unique healing process. It doesn't matter what you've experienced in the past or the pain you've caused other people. Your healing journey will certainly not be easy, but when you get to the other side you'll look back and see how the Lord reframed your brokenness into a place of strength and beauty which will then carry you through any difficulty you face during the rest of your life.

I heard a podcast a while back (I can't remember who hosted it) which described the cracks from our brokenness as beautiful opportunities for the Lord's light to shine through us so others can see Him in a tangible way. Another spiritual principle the Lord reinforced through my experience is the importance of loving people where they are regardless of their choices. Throughout the worst of my brokenness I was not capable of doing that until the Lord began healing me and supplied HIS strength to rise above my circumstances to choose love rather than reacting to what was happening around me.

If you are currently in a long-term season of brokenness, take a minute to say the following prayer:

Lord, my circumstances feel like they will never end, and my brokenness sits heavy on my chest like a 500 lb. weight. I'm exhausted, angry, and ready to give up on you. I want to trust you. I want to believe you are working all things out for good. Please, Lord, open my eyes and ears, and send me a sign that you haven't forgotten about me. Give me a glimpse of hope that I will eventually experience beauty from my ashes. I believe you can do that, Lord, and will commit to looking and listening for that sign because I know you love me more than I can imagine.

Okay, now take a few deep breaths and imagine the Lord saying this to you as a declaration of commitment to what you just prayed: *Beloved child, whatever you ask for in my name, trust that you are receiving it and it will be yours* (Mark 11:24).

The Lord may take a week, a month or even a few years to answer that prayer, but eventually He will. I promise! You will see your brokenness become beautiful in His perfect timing and in His perfect way.

Chapter 2 - Jehovah Jireh Reigns

<u>July 10</u>

It's been just over a week since I made the decision to accept the Lord's invitation to go on an Adventure with Him.

Since then it's been a whirlwind of activity arranging to store my motorcycle with a friend, coordinating mail and other things with my Dad, alerting friends and family of estimated timelines for when I may be in their area, and mentally reviewing all of my stuff to determine what I need to pack in my car and what I can live without.

As I was doing all this planning, it suddenly occurred to me that my 18-year-old car would need to be serviced to make sure it was safe to travel across the country for an unspecified amount of time. With limited financial resources, I knew it was going to be interesting to cover that cost along with the other bills coming due in the next two weeks. But I also knew the Lord invited me on this trip, which meant I could trust He was going before me to prepare whatever I needed (Ps 139:5). Yesterday those provisions began.

I went online to see what auto service centers were in the area and checked for coupons. Within 15-minutes I found a "Summer Road Trip Check-up" special for only $14.95 which included a 23-point safety checklist.

I dropped my car off and went for a walk. When I returned they provided several suggested service items, all of which were not necessary except for the tires. They said the front two were bald and the back two weren't much better, suggesting a tire shop on the other side of town. The cost of four new tires was way more than I had to spend, but I trusted the Lord would figure it out. I went back online to look for more coupons and make calls to see what my options were.

After 30-minutes of contacting various tire stores in the area, the lowest price I could find was still more than I could afford. I decided to call up the Consultant I do work *for to clarify the date of my next paycheck in order to juggle money accordingly. After sharing my tire dilemma, he suggested purchasing quality used tires and also checking a different part of metro-Atlanta since the area I was currently staying tended to be overpriced.*

I googled used tire shops in another part of metro-Atlanta, made a few calls, and the only one who answered the phone gave me a deal I couldn't pass up. I arranged to stop by first thing the next morning. As I went to bed, I reminded the Lord that I trusted Him - even though I saw no realistic way to pay for both my upcoming bills and the tires - and asked Him to miraculously provide a way to make it all happen.

I arrived at the tire store early and hung out until they opened. After the mechanic arrived and I told him what I needed, he walked over to my car, took one look at my tires and with righteous anger said, "These tires don't need to be replaced....who told you that? Look at your treads, do they look bald to you?" I responded sheepishly because I've never been able to clearly tell bald from good tire treads. He looked me straight in the eye and said he was not going to take my money for something I didn't need, unlike other shops who would take it just to make a buck.

I thanked the mechanic profusely, told him the Lord would bless his integrity, and asked him to rotate the tires since I knew they needed at least that much done. After I paid for the rotation, I handed him a $5 bill to buy a coffee or beer on me (I wished I had a larger bill in my wallet, because I would've gladly given him more to reward his honesty!).

My prayers were answered! Jehovah Jireh had definitely gone before me to lead me to the right mechanic in order to provide a miraculous turnaround as His testimony of continual provision in exchange for my heart and my will surrendered to Him.

Did the Lord fix my tires overnight as I lay sleeping or did the first mechanic just make a mistake? Who cares!! All I know is the Lord took care of it, and He can do that anyway He pleases! As I drove away from the tire shop you better believe the heavens heard me praising the Lord in a mighty way! :)

Whenever I surrender my finances and my future to the Lord, it gives Him the opportunity to bless me in ways I can't even imagine (Eph 3:20) and I know the blessings will keep coming as long as I step out in faith each day from this point forward!

My car is now ready for the trip. All I have left to do is take the stuff I don't need to the storage unit. Based on what happened today with the car, I know it's going to be an amazing Adventure!

Chapter 3 - You Shall Have No Idols

July 12

A few weeks ago, before I had made the decision to go on the Adventure with the Lord, one of my big hesitations in saying yes was the inconvenience of having to live out of my car and sleep in a different place night after night.

The Lord loves me too much to allow me to stay in a mindset that isn't serving me well, so it didn't take too long for Him to convict me of my "comfort and convenience" idol. Idol may be an odd word to use, but if you think about it, *anything* we value more than the Lord and *anything* that prevents us from following the Lord's will for our lives is essentially a modern-day idol. Even our feelings can be idols if they get in the way.

Here's how that conviction happened: For days I had been wrestling with the Lord, trying to wrap my head around His "crazy" road trip request and really hoping I had totally misheard His invitation. After all, the Lord knows I rarely ever sleep through the night because I'm such a light sleeper…especially when I'm on a couch out in the open rather than in a spare bedroom with the illusion of being in my own space.

Just thinking about having to spend an unknown number of weeks or months bouncing from couch to couch, or potentially sleeping in my car from time to time, was not appealing to me. Not only that, with my unstable financial situation how would I pay for meals and gas on the trip?

A day or so later as I was going through emails, a video from Bethel Church in CA caught my eye. It was titled, "Shifting Spiritual Atmospheres" with Dawna DeSilva. The moment I saw it I knew the Lord wanted me to watch the video. It was chock full of fantastic information. Then right near the end, the Lord lovingly sucker-punched me. I don't exactly remember what Dawna said, but the message was basically this (in my *words): "What are you holding tightly to in your life that could be an obstacle to what the Lord wants for your life?"*

Man!!!! The Lord knows how to accurately shoot a truth arrow straight into my heart!

That moment was probably the first time I knew this trip was going to happen, even though I wasn't ready to accept it just yet. As that question resonated within my heart and soul, my eyes started tearing. I immediately repented at valuing comfort and convenience more than the Lord's will for my life. I quickly asked Him to forgive me, and requested His help to lay those desires down as I considered accepting his Adventure invitation. It took a few days to process through my feelings before peace around the trip showed up more consistently.

Fast-forward to now and my attitude is completely different. It's been so much fun sharing my upcoming Adventure with friends and family, and making plans to "couch surf" as I travel throughout the country. One of the best planning conversations I had via text was with Becca, one of my New York Youth For Christ (YFC) kids from back in 1987. I unofficially adopted her and her brother, Ray, at the same time their Mom adopted me as a member of their family when I was running a YFC club at their home.

I was 20 at the time, Becca was 13 and I think Ray was 12. The first memory they have of me is setting up a flag football game with all the YFC kids and playfully running Ray over to get to the goal line (or at least that's how I remember it). Ray couldn't believe a girl beat him and I just laughed because most people have always underestimated my determination and inner strength to accomplish whatever I set out to do. Ray, Becca and I became fast friends and "family" that day. We've stayed in touch all these years, just like I've stayed in touch with my Indiana YFC kids when I worked there in 1990.

The reason my conversation with Becca was so amazing was because the Lord used her to remind me, once again, He goes before me to prepare my way. I totally forgot she started a non-profit years ago called "Dirty Kid Couch-surfing Coalition" to assist homeless and transient youth in finding shelter, transportation and friendship as they travel across the U.S. Becca told me she had connections all across the country and said to let her know if I needed a place to stay so she could check her database for a reputable host who would consider taking me in for a night even though I'm not homeless.

How cool is that? Thirty-years ago I was taking care of her and now she's taking care of me! I love how the Lord arranges things like that to bless me. As I've contacted all my YFC "kids" about my Adventure travel plans, they can't wait to see me and have all offered their homes to hang out for a few days as I pass through their areas.

I have a few other planned stops with people I know, but most of my trip is uncertain. I have no idea where I'll be staying or what situations I may run into. Yet, I trust the Lord will provide a safe place every night regardless of whether it's on a couch, in a spare room, or even in my car. Not to mention, as I find Celebrate Recovery meetings along my route who have openings for testimony speakers, my hope is that they will consider hosting me for a night along my travels.

One thing I am certain of is the Lord would never have invited me on this "crazy" Adventure if He wasn't setting me up for something amazing in the next season of my life. When the Lord calls someone into a higher position of authority and responsibility in His kingdom, the preparation challenges are generally more difficult than normal to ensure they learn what they need to learn in order to succeed.

I know my Adventure journey is an equipping and sanctification period for the spiritual mantles He's going to give me and the new anointing that's coming. This entire trip seems to be designed to deepen my faith and develop a deeper intimacy with Him.

I anticipate the trip won't always be smooth and am guessing the Lord is going to allow the enemy to set up some difficult challenges for me along the way to refine my character and give me opportunities to use the spiritual gifts and natural skills I've developed throughout my life for His glory and my growth. Though I'm not really looking forward to those moments, I know the Lord will always provide a way through it (Philippians 4:19 / Psalm 115:11-12), and I'll be better for it when I get to the other side.

Chapter 4 - 1ˢᵗ Day On The Road

<u>*July 24*</u>

Last week was a flurry of activity complete with a variety of emotions as I packed everything I owned to determine what I needed and what I could leave behind in storage. Not knowing the time frame I'd be gone added to the challenge of sorting everything into "keep" and "leave" piles.

My car is a 2000 Toyota Corolla. I spent a lot of time staring at it trying to figure out the best way to organize everything in the small trunk, the floor of the front passenger seat, and on one side of the back seat just in case I had to lay down the other front bucket seat to sleep in my car on a night I had no place to stay. Thankfully my previous history of numerous moves and my Tetris packing skills gave me an edge to fit everything into my car. I locked the storage unit and headed over to house sit for a friend for two days before I left on my Adventure.

The morning of 7/22/Sun I got in my car at 7 AM excited about the Adventure and curious as to what I would experience over the next few weeks or months since I had no idea how long the Lord would keep me on the road. My odometer read 232,188 and I wondered what it would read when I got back. One thing I knew was that my 18-year-old car would certainly get a workout!

Six hours later, Raleigh, NC was my first stop to visit with an old college friend and his wife (Greg & Beth). We had not seen each other in five years, and enjoyed swapping stories, catching each other up on our lives, and making each other laugh at the things we had learned along the way.

After a wonderful meal it was time to head out for my next stop in Chapel Hill, NC to see my Aunt and Uncle (it's been about three years since I've seen either of them). After a great reunion, I went to bed peaceful and thankful for the amazing relationships I have been blessed to have throughout my life.

As I look out the window of my Aunt's home this morning, I am very aware that my landscape is going to change daily throughout this Adventure. Almost every day I'm going to be in a different place and wake up to a new horizon with only partial knowledge of what's coming next.

What I do know so far is this: Tuesday I am heading to Pennsylvania to see a friend, Wednesday I'm speaking at a Celebrate Recovery meeting in central PA, Thursday I'm seeing my nephew with a possible CR testimony that night, and Friday yet another Celebrate Recovery in northern New Jersey. Saturday I have a high school event and then on Sunday I will visit with another high school friend. The following week is a mystery. Only the Lord knows, and I trust He'll show me where to go when I need to know it.

I can clearly see how the Lord used this last year of healing and recovery, along with learning how to surrender on a deeper level to live life "one day at a time," as a foundation to prepare me for this trip. Had I not learned those lessons, I would not have been capable of stepping out into the unknown on this Adventure with confidence and courage.

I still occasionally look up at the sky and remind the Lord, "This is the craziest thing you've ever asked me to do." I know He's laughing back at me in a fatherly way. Similar to a Professor working with a Graduate Student who wants to excel in their field, the Lord has uniquely designed this trip to stretch me to my limits and set me up for success in the next season of my life.

Thanks to all of you who have texted, emailed or sent messages on Facebook to let me know you are praying for me, and for all the other well wishes. I truly appreciate you and am thankful for your intercession as I travel.

I'll continue to update you on my Adventure to let you know how things are going. Until then, blessings to you and don't forget to keep your eyes open for all the amazing things the Lord is doing around you too!

:) ~Kris

Chapter 5 - "Acts" Is Lifestyle & Mindset!

My Holy Spirit led Adventure is the wildest thing I've ever experienced, including all the Holy Spirit provision I received each mile of the trip. And yet that journey fully aligns with the unorthodox path the Lord has had me on for quite a while.

Sometime in my late 20s I began to see significant differences between the lives of Jesus followers in the U.S.A. and those in other parts of the world. Stories of miracles, signs and wonders occurring in other countries fascinated me. However, like most Believers, I had no frame of reference for those experiences being available to me as well.

I grew up in a Protestant culture, attending various church denominations until the Lord led me to a Messianic Jewish-Gentile congregation later in life. My faith experience from childhood produced a distinct presumption that supernatural experiences were a thing of the past. Miraculous healings, divine signs and wonders were to be investigated thoroughly; considered suspect until validated – which was unlikely - because things like that just didn't happen in my world.

In my early 40s the Lord began to speak to my heart through various blogs and books He led me to, prompting me to reconsider that perspective. Over time my heart started to soften, replacing immediate suspicion with curiosity at what I was learning. Of course, all of that was happening on a subconscious level. I certainly wasn't seeking to experience the supernatural power of the Holy Spirit. I was just very intrigued at the information I was exposed to.

Then three years ago everything changed! The Lord began to put people in my circle of friends and professional relationships who told stories of how the Lord gave them Words of Knowledge and Prophetic Prayers for people they didn't know who crossed their path; how the Lord prompted them to pray for healing and seeing it occur before their eyes; and other stories of people tapping into Holy Spirit power with supernatural results on a regular basis. Because I knew these people well, I could not dismiss their testimonies. All I could do was marvel at what they experienced and wonder why it didn't happen around me.

A few months later the Lord led me to a series of Holy Spirit focused documentaries by Darren Wilson that totally rocked my world: *Finger of God, Holy Ghost, Holy Ghost Reborn, Father of Lights,* and *Furious Love* (you can rent or purchase a streaming version of those movies at www.wpfilm.com for a very reasonable price).

Slowly but surely, because of my sincere desire to understand and experience that level of Holy Spirit anointing, the Lord began to open my eyes and lead me to opportunities to witness it personally until I was able to finally say with certainty, "I was blind, but now I see!" (John 9:25b).

The following year the Lord led me to a Council of Leaders group in Georgia consisting of professional men and women from various faith backgrounds and life experiences who were dedicated to stewarding everything the Lord gave them (personally and professionally) for Kingdom impact within their sphere of influence. Most of the members had learned to hear from the Lord in a prophetic way and prayed prophetically whenever someone requested it. The Lord set up that group and the friendships I've made since then to become the catalyst for the next stage of my spiritual development.

I remember the first time I attended the Council of Leaders meeting. I was not sure what to expect, but fully confident the Lord wanted me to be there. Bill, the Council leader, began the meeting by having everyone introduce themselves followed by a discussion on a Kingdom impact topic. Those conversations were like a breath of fresh air. Everyone was comfortable sharing their life stories and confidently transparent about their challenges and the struggles within those difficult situations. At the end of the discussion they opened the group to a dedicated time of prophetic prayer for anyone who wanted it.

I was so eager to experience my first prophetic prayer that I immediately said yes. That particular day there were only four people plus myself (afterwards I learned there are typically anywhere from 5 -15 people at any given meeting). Of the four people, one was my Dad (it was his first time too); I had never met Sherri & Wayne before, and Bill and I had only met once for coffee a few days earlier which is how I got invited to the Council meeting.

To honor the Lord, the process the group uses for prophetic prayer is to have someone start out with a general prayer for the Lord to help the group tune into His Spirit. Then everyone silently listens for the Lord to give them words of knowledge, scripture passages, visions, or any sort of encouragement for the specific person being prayed for. The group does not generally know what is going on that person's life except what that person shared in the introductions segment.

During introductions that day I had shared only a snippet of the long-term challenge which had caused so much brokenness in my life over the past few years. As I listened to the general prayer Sherri gave before the group began to pray for me, I heard glimpses of prophetic knowledge and was curious as to what else the Lord would say to them about my circumstances and my future. After a few moments of silence, one by one, Bill, Sherri and then Wayne began sharing what the Lord told them. Everything they said was from a place of love, grace, edification, and encouragement.

Tears began flowing from my eyes as I recognized the Lord demonstrating His Holy Spirit anointing through each member of the group. Other than my Dad, no one else could have known the information they shared or the context in which they shared it except through the Lord's guidance. Their prayers rang clear as a bell because I had the background information required to accurately interpret what the Lord told them.

After everyone was done praying for me, I took a few minutes to share a bit more of what was going on in my life to confirm the information the Lord gave them. The entire experience of receiving accurate prophetic prayer was amazing. By the end of that meeting I knew this group would be the next step in my Holy Spirit training process.

For the first time in my life I finally understood why Paul encouraged the gift of prophesy in his letter to the Corinthians: *"Pursue love, and earnestly desire the spiritual gifts, especially that you may prophesy"* (1 Corinthians 14:1 / ESV); and also in his letter to the Romans:: *"Having gifts that differ according to the grace given to us, let us use them: if prophecy, in proportion to our faith; if service, in our serving; the one who teaches, in his teaching; the one who exhorts, in his exhortation; the one who contributes, in generosity; the one who leads, with zeal; the one who does acts of mercy, with cheerfulness"* (Romans 12:6-8 / ESV).

Over the next year I attended almost every Council meeting and saw my prophetic gifts develop to become more accurate over time as someone would say to me something like, "Kris when you said X, you were dead on and here's what that meant....or, when you saw X, you absolutely confirmed what the Lord told me previously."

I also learned that when a bunch of people are prophetically praying with pure intentions to hear from the Lord, that the skill level of everyone in the group rises to the level of the person most gifted in the room. It's like being in a car behind a fast-moving tractor trailer. The closer you get, the more draft you pick up from the truck, which in turn makes your car go faster without having to step on the gas. My prophetic accuracy and clarity were generally much stronger when I was at the Council meeting than when I was by myself prophetically praying for someone.

Of course, like any new training ground, sometimes what I said or saw prophetically had a flat landing. And that's okay too because the Lord tells us, "*Do not quench the Spirit. Do not despise prophecies, but test everything; hold fast to what is good. Abstain from every form of evil*" (1 Thessalonians 5:19-21 / ESV). Another scripture also warns us: "*Beloved, do not believe every spirit, but test the spirits to see whether they are from God, for many false prophets have gone out into the world*. (1 John 4:1 / ESV)."

We all have filters through which we process information. In a prophetic environment, each member of the group has a desire to hear accurately from the Lord, but sometimes we may speak things from our heart rather than from His Spirit. It's not that we are being a false prophet, but that our heart gets ahead of the Lord. I learned the rollercoaster of "hit and miss" is absolutely normal when developing the gift of prophesy. Like any new skill, we must be willing to practice continuously until consistent (not perfect) accuracy becomes the norm.

One of the things I love about the Council group is their maturity in the prophetic process and their commitment to create an environment of safety to ensure prophetic words and visions are delivered in a loving, edifying and encouraging way. They also give everyone permission to discard anything spoken that they didn't connect to. We always record prayers on our individual phones so we have an accurate record of what was said to take with us. I generally listen to the recording a few times, transcribe it, and then pray over the information before discarding any part of it in case the prayer is a glimpse of what's coming rather than what I know today (which is usually the case).

If your interest is peaked and you want to learn more about how to develop your skill in prophetic prayer, there are great resources from well-known prophetic trainers such as Graham Cooke, Shawn Boltz, James W. Goll, and Kris Vallotton. If you go to their websites, they have online stores to purchase materials to begin that journey (see Resources Section in the back of this book).

After undergoing focused Holy Spirit training for more than a year and witnessing several supernatural experiences, the Lord began to show me that *Acts was not just a book in the Bible, but rather a lifestyle and mindset every Believer should aspire to because of the Holy Spirit they carry inside them.*

The Old and New Testament describes many supernatural experiences occurring in the lives of people who maintained deeply intimate relationships with the Lord. That intimacy allowed the Holy Spirit to flow through them in a powerful way, and that same anointed power is available to us every day through the Holy Spirit. Don't ever doubt that because doubt is one of the devil's greatest weapons to slow people down or keep them permanently stuck from accessing the gifts and the purpose the Lord truly desires for their lives.

I love how Crystal Wade, founder of Hope Streams, explains the accessibility of the power of the Holy Spirit in her blog post titled "How to Open Your Door Between Heaven and Earth."[3] She says, "Jesus revealed that the Kingdom of God is inside us (Luke 17:21). When He walked the earth, He stayed open as a door - a passageway between Heaven and Earth. He released the Kingdom of God from His Spirit, His inner man, to the outer world. Jesus, as a door, was fully open to our Father in Heaven and fully open to us on Earth. Through Him, Father worked freely. We too are doors. For most of us, our doors are not as open as Jesus' were. The good news is, that ball is in our court."

Wade then suggests four ways we can open those doors and declares, "Each time we move through this process, our doors open wider!"

1. Keep bringing wounds to Him to heal instead of burying or carrying them, so that our door between Heaven and Earth, inside us, opens wider.

2. Look honestly within and confess the judgments, unforgiveness and bitterness we've held against Him for the troubles we and our families have been through.

3. Comply with conditions for the heavenly Kingdom's palace doors to open by separating ourselves from that which our Father calls unclean, so we can have

---

[3] Wade, Crystal, How to Open Your Door Between Heaven and Earth, http://elijahlist.com/words/display_word.html?ID=21195

deep fellowship with Him which Jesus paid for on the cross.

4. Allow Him to build compassion and love that does the best for others. Most of the wounds we've received came from His process through our trials and sufferings, intended to yield compassion and love in us.

I've read the entire Bible several times throughout my life. At different points in my spiritual growth I glean more truth as new revelations leap off the page. In my recent season of spiritual awakening, so many verses I merely glossed over in my younger years have suddenly become alive as I walk in new awareness of the Holy Spirit-filled life the Lord wants all of us to live.

For instance, Matthew 10:5-13 (ESV) says, *"These twelve Jesus sent out, instructing them, "Go nowhere among the Gentiles and enter no town of the Samaritans, but go rather to the lost sheep of the house of Israel. And proclaim as you go, saying, 'The kingdom of heaven is at hand.' Heal the sick, raise the dead, cleanse lepers, cast out demons. You received without paying; give without pay. Acquire no gold or silver or copper for your belts, no bag for your journey, or two tunics or sandals or a staff, for the laborer deserves his food. And whatever town or village you enter, find out who is worthy in it and stay there until you depart. As you enter the house, greet it. And if the house is worthy, let your peace come upon it, but if it is not worthy, let your peace return to you."*

The original 12 disciples were just as human as we are today. The Lord sent them out with a command to have faith enough to heal the sick, raise the dead, cleanse lepers, and cast out demons. Today we have access to the same Holy Spirit power they had to do the same. All that's required is to deepen your relationship with the Lord to receive His anointing power in proportion to your intimacy with Him.

You may be wondering if I have healed the sick, raised the dead, cleansed lepers, or cast out demons. Through inner healing and deliverance prayers I've been using over the last few years, I believe I am having an impact on casting out demons in my personal life and my family line (if you are unaware, everyone has had demonic activity attached to them at some point in their life through generational sins or open doors of sin you've allowed in by the choices you made, but have not yet repented of from your past).

I recently had an opportunity to heal the sick - my first time ever! The Lord graciously set up that situation for me in response to a prayer asking Him to increase my holy spirit anointing as described in Matthew 10. It wasn't a dramatic healing experience, but because she was instantly healed it helped my faith rise to the next level in that area of my spiritual development. Here's that story:

A friend was having neck pain and unable to turn her neck at a normal radius on both sides. It had been that way for a few days and nothing she tried to alleviate the pain had worked. She was resigned to just dealing with it and put a sticky heating pad on her neck to reduce some of the discomfort. As she was sharing that with me, I felt the Lord prompt me to pray for her to be healed. I honestly didn't have enough faith at that moment, so I tucked that thought into the back of my head and decided to wait until later that day to see how she was doing. Of course, the Lord would not let me get away with that, so her neck remained the same all day. Later she and I were talking about my Adventure when I realized I was dishonoring my friend, and the Lord, by NOT offering to pray for her to be healed.

I asked my friend a few clarification questions to get a gauge for her pain level and the location of the pain, placed my hand on that area and prayed something like: "Lord, I come before you with a mustard seed of faith - which is all I need to gain access to your healing power. I command all pain to leave her neck. I call forth a healthier version of her neck to replace the out of alignment version she is experiencing currently. I command the muscles and bones in her neck to adjust back to full health right now. In Jesus' name and by His blood. Amen."

I didn't feel anything while I was praying which is why I was surprised to see my friend looking at me with astonishment. She moved her neck from side to side, up and down, and said the moment I spoke the word "neck" she felt a cooling sensation filter throughout her neck area, despite the heating pad still had on her neck. We were both amazed, and I was in shock that the prayer actually worked. <u>Oh, ME, of little faith</u>!!! (a personal twist on Matthew 8:26). The rest of the day she kept checking her neck and it was indeed healed. We praised the Lord many times for His willingness to honor my mustard seed faith prayer.

Regarding the other two commands from Jesus in Matthew 10, I have not yet had an opportunity to raise the dead or cleanse a leper. Faith, in any proportion, is a starting point for the Lord to do those types of miracles through us. Therefore, I know there's a greater likelihood I will experience the opportunity to do both of those things at some point in my life if I keep developing my faith in those areas (though I'm guessing I may fumble around and possibly even freeze the first time it happens).

Another passage of scripture that popped for me over the last year is Acts 2:17 (ESV): "And in the last days it shall be, God declares, that *I will pour out my Spirit on all flesh, and your sons and your daughters shall prophesy, and your young men shall see visions, and your old men shall dream dreams; even on my male servants and female servants in those days I will pour out my Spirit, and they shall prophesy.*"

Finally, Acts 2:42-47 (ESV) says, "And they devoted themselves to the apostles' teaching and the fellowship, to the breaking of bread and the prayers. *And awe came upon every soul, and many wonders and signs were being done through the apostles. And all who believed were together and had all things in common.* And they were selling their possessions and belongings and distributing the proceeds to all, as any had need. And day by day, attending the temple together and breaking bread in their homes, they received their food with glad and generous hearts, praising God and having favor with all the people. And the Lord added to their number day by day those who were being saved."

Now that is a community of people I would love to know! Their lives were so transformed by the Gospel message, they willingly surrendered everything they had in a communal atmosphere for everyone's benefit. Gladness, generosity, and favor became the cultural atmosphere with every new group of Believers, and signs and wonders became a "normal" part of the disciples' ministry to everyone around them.

We may not have that exact type of experience today, but I'll bet my life we could come close if we were all willing to commit to developing the intimacy required to access the gifts and power the Lord provides through the Holy Spirit within us.

Are you brave enough to take that leap of faith? If so, would you stop a minute and say this prayer?

Lord Jesus you are King of Kings, Great High Priest, Prince of Peace, and my Redeemer. Your word says that when the disciples asked for an increase in their faith in Luke 17, you responded that the smallest dose of faith - even as small as a grain of mustard seed - would result in their ability to access the power to uproot a mulberry tree and plant it in the sea. I believe that promise is still valid today and humbly ask you to increase my faith. I want to deepen my intimacy with you to gain access to all the Holy Spirit gifts you promised to those who accept you as Messiah.

I want Acts to become more than just a book in the Bible in my world. I desire Acts to become a lifestyle and mindset within me. Lord Jesus, bring the right people into my life to mentor me into a deeply intimate relationship with you, and lead me to the best resources to develop all the spiritual gifts the early church experienced as a normal part of their life.

I recognize praying this prayer will most likely prompt the enemy to attack me in ways I can't even imagine because He knows my growing intimacy with you will cause him to lose ground in multiple places within my sphere of influence. I am prepared to trust you to provide whatever I need to overcome those attacks. I am fully willing to undergo the pruning process required to develop my character into who I need to become to receive the gifts you promised, along with the wisdom required for maximum Kingdom Impact.

Lord, as it says in 2 Corinthians 7:1 (CJB), "….let us purify ourselves from everything that can defile either body or spirit, and strive to be completely holy, out of reverence for God." I willingly undergo purification out of reverence for the purpose you have for my life. Thank you in advance,

Lord, for giving me access to everything I need to grow into the [man / woman] you want me to become.

I love you, Lord, and look forward to experiencing an Acts Lifestyle and Mindset as you transform me from the inside out into your likeness throughout my lifetime. Amen!

Fantastic! Now I want you to solidify this prayer by finding the live version of the song, "Miracles" by Jesus Culture on YouTube. Take time today to sit in the Lord's presence and sing this song to Him as full declaration of your belief. Then keep your eyes open over the next few months for opportunities He will present to you to partner with Him as a step of faith to experience the Holy Spirit in action in whatever miracles He wants to do through you.

When something does happen - even if it's just a small step - email me at Kris @ BeginToShift.com to tell me the story so I can rejoice with you! I can't wait to see how the Lord shows up and shows off in your life!!

Two other suggestions I'd like to make are:

1. Subscribe to the "Exploring the Prophetic" podcast with Shawn Boltz on iTunes. You'll hear story after story from people of all walks of life who are guided by the Holy Spirit, and the remarkable things that happened as they followed the Lord's leading in all kinds of situations.

2. In the Bible read John chapters 14 -17. Jesus provides a lot of information about the Holy Spirit in those verses.

May Jesus' words in John 16:13-15 (ESV) become a reality in your life today: *"When the Spirit of truth comes, he will guide you into all the truth, for he will not speak on his own authority, but whatever he hears he will speak, and he will declare to you the things that are to come. He will glorify me, for he will take what is mine and declare it to you. All that the Father has is mine; therefore I said that he will take what is mine and declare it to you."*

Chapter 6 - I LOVE NY!

<u>*July 27*</u>

Hi all! Today's post is a video. Check out the word on the huge truck behind me as it passes by (I didn't even see it until I watched the video later that day).

I love it when the Lord sends a personal message to show me He's pleased I'm not letting anything steal my joy on this trip!

Sorry the video is a bit jumpy. It's the first time I've used my phone to make a video. I'll do a better job of holding it steady the next time I create one.

Blessings and favor to you! Have a great rest of your day!

To access Video link, go to:
http://BeginToShift.com/crazy-blessing-videos

Chapter 7 - Joy

August 1

Since arriving in the NJ-NY area on 7/28/Sat I have had so many memories run through my head while driving down roads I haven't been on since childhood and being with people I haven't seen in a very long time.

I had forgotten how rural this part of the country is with all the narrow twisting roads up and down hills and mountains. Every time I shifted my car from 4th to 3rd to 2nd gear around a sharp turn, I recalled the motorcycle rides I attended back in 2001 when I first bought my bike.

In my last blog (the I Love NY video) I mentioned that the devil was messin' with me, but I wasn't letting him steal my joy. Here are the stories I was referring to in that video:

On 7/25/Wed as I neared Jonesboro, PA to speak at a Celebrate Recovery meeting that evening I was really tired from driving in the rain over the past few days in addition to all the early morning departures from everywhere else I had stayed. At one point during the drive to Jonesboro I pulled over at a large church to take a nap in their back parking lot. Forty-five minutes later when I tried to start the car, all I heard was silence. The battery had died and I had no idea why because I had turned the car off.

Knowing the Lord was all over this trip, I decided I wasn't going to stress over it and walked around to the front of the church to ask whomever was there to jump my car. The Pastor offered to do so, and we had a nice conversation about my Adventure as we walked to my car. After the car successfully started, we discovered I had forgotten to turn off the lights when I took my nap (they had been on all morning because of the rain) causing the battery to die. I thanked the Pastor for his time and before I headed out, I prayed for both he and his church. Once I was sure everything in the car was working correctly, I continued onward to the home of the CR couple who was going to host me that evening.

An hour later I arrived at my host's home. As I began to get my stuff out of the car and close my windows due to rain and flood warnings in the area, to my surprise the driver's side power window went up, but the front passenger window would not move from the half way position. I kept pressing the "up" button and still no movement, so my host was nice enough to let me park the car in the garage to avoid having my stuff get wet.

Because rain was in the forecast for days in every direction, we stopped at Walmart to get a tarp to protect my car anywhere it was parked during my travels until I could get it fixed. Meanwhile I was doing mental gymnastics trying to figure out how to keep the rain out without the tarp when I was driving because I needed to see the mirror through the passenger window. Once again, I refused to allow the situation to stress me out and told the devil he wasn't going to steal my joy.

Trusting the Lord to take care of my car, I drove to the Jonesboro CR that evening and wrapped the tarp around passenger door before I locked up the car. About 20-minutes later there was a torrential down-pour for over an hour. The Lord timed it perfectly for me to take care of the car before I went inside. I was so thankful because I would have been a soaking mess during my testimony if the rain had started any earlier.

Because I wouldn't let the devil steal my joy during all the challenges I faced that day, I was able to remain relaxed and fully present to serve the men and women in the CR program that night. After my testimony several people thanked me for sharing my story as an encouragement to their individual situations.

After the program ended it was very dark outside and still lightly raining, making it hard to see while driving. I told my host I would follow her to the Home Depot near her home and then head back to her place when I was done so I could look for clear plastic to put over the window that wasn't working to protect my stuff while driving if the rain was really bad the next morning.

I pulled out behind her and got caught at a light a few miles later. I watched my host turn left and pull her *black car into a gas station to wait for me. When the light changed I turned left and saw a black car waiting to exit the gas station, so I let it in and proceeded to follow behind it. After about 15-minutes of going on roads that didn't look familiar from the route we took earlier to the CR meeting, I saw the black car pull into a driveway which was not my host's home.*

I knew my host had a friend in her car and assumed it was the other woman's home, but after waiting several minutes and not seeing her car leave the house I began wondering what was taking so long. Then I took a really good look at the black car realizing it was not my host's vehicle! It seems I had followed the wrong black car at the gas station (I hope you are laughing, because I did as soon as I noticed it).

I told the devil once again, he was not going to steal my joy, and set the GPS to head back to my host's home. By this time it was raining even harder. Rural roads in the rain are hard enough to drive on in the daytime, never mind at night. After what seemed like an eternity of right and left turns on roads I couldn't see well, I was beginning to get concerned that I would never find the Home Depot (it was near her house, but I didn't have an address). After 15-minutes of driving around I finally saw the store in my rear-view mirror.

After a quick U-turn I noticed the entrance to the Home Depot was on the other side of the road. It was still pouring and I couldn't see well, so I turned left and was thankful I had finally arrived. The next thing I know there are cars heading right for me beeping like crazy! It seems I had mistakenly turned onto a one-way street!

I knew the Lord would protect me so I remained calm, stayed as far to the right as I could knowing the entrance was only about 40-feet ahead, and said I was sorry several times to the drivers even though they couldn't hear me. I drove straight to the pickup overhang, parked the car out of the rain, hid all the valuables just in case someone decided to take advantage of an open window, and went inside.

It took 20-minutes and two Home Depot staff to brainstorm the best solution for my open window. I purchased flexible clear window protector sheets and duct-tape. By now it was close to 11 PM. I was very tired and just wanted to go to bed, so I left the window alone, drove to my host's home, pulled the car into the garage and went inside. My host asked me what happened because she didn't know where my car was after the light, and I told her the story of following someone I thought was her along with the one-way road mistake. We both had a good laugh about it.

The next morning I headed north to visit my nephew. I left at 6:30 AM very happy the weather was clear and cool rather than rainy. I spent most of my drive time praising and worshiping the Lord, proclaiming He would provide a solution to my car window problem without it costing me all the cash in my wallet. A few minutes later I felt the Lord say, "Did you check the child safety lock?" I looked down, pressed the button, and Wha-la! The window went up! WHOO HOO! I never use the child-lock button, so it never even occurred to me to check it. I'm sure the devil knew that and used it to do his best to interfere with my trip. Epic failure on his part!!!   :)

A recurring lesson throughout this Adventure seems to be this: when I surrender EVERYTHING to the Lord, I don't have to stress because I can trust the Lord will provide a way through my circumstances, which allows me to feel peaceful each day no matter what comes my way.

After visiting my nephew, I drove just over three hours to give my testimony at the CR in Middletown, NY. After the program, one of the ladies said the timing of my testimony was divine because she had been asking the Lord that week for a sign about her circumstances. We chatted a bit and then later in the conversation the Lord gave her a prophetic word for me that was so precious.

Because I don't know where I'll be staying when I get back to Atlanta, and because I am currently living out of my car during the Adventure, I jokingly told her that I'm a bit homeless these days as I travel from place to place. After I said those words, she looked up and then directly at me. With a smile she said the Lord told her to tell me, "You are not homeless, not homeless. For the heaven is the Lord's and the earth His footstool. So in the days ahead as you go from one place to the next, know that you are not homeless. You are just moving about and around in His house."

WOW! What a powerful word from the Lord to remind me that I am never out of His sight, and that each place I step is on His land with full authority as His Ambassador throughout this Adventure! I am so thankful the Lord blessed me with those encouraging words to not be concerned because He's taking care of my future living situation even though I have no idea how yet!

I'm heading northwest from here to visit with one of my former Youth for Christ (YFC) "kids" and then I'll be speaking at another CR a few days later in western NY.

I hope you are having a great week! I'll post more about my Adventure when I have time. :)

Chapter 8 - Memory Lane

By the time this is published I will be just about two weeks into my Adventure. Up to this point I have visited NC (Raleigh and Chapel Hill), NJ (Sussex), PA (Jonesboro, Lebanon, Coal Township, Milford, Genesee) and NY (Middletown, Unionville, Westtown, Otisville, Endicott, Alfred, Houghton, Wellsville, Rochester and Buffalo). I still have a few more stops to go in NY, back to PA, then off to IN.

There have been too many memory lane moments to count throughout this trip including seeing a Friendly's restaurant and immediately turning around to have a Fribble shake like I used to do as a kid during many hot summer evenings with my family….yummy!

Later I took a detour to drive past the first house my parents bought when I was in Kindergarten followed by a stop in Westtown for an informal high school class get together. It was fun to catch up with everyone after 20+ years. Over the weekend I stayed with two different high school friends and was also able to have dinner with my brother, Todd.

From there I drove about two hours to visit Ray, my former NY Youth For Christ (YFC) kid. During one of our conversations he reminded me of the time he and his sister, Becca, came to NYC when I lived there; and another time I drove to the airport in Atlanta to pick him up on a long layover when he was in the Marines. The entire visit was fantastic, and I loved finally meeting his wife, Lisa, after so many years of hearing about her.

The next day I drove about 150 miles further west to see Ray's sister, Becca. We spent the day walking around my old college campus which is where I first got in involved in YFC. Becca reminded me about the pizza and milkshake moments we shared back then when she and Ray used to visit me on campus, and how much fun we all had when I would stay over at their home to hang out late into the night.

Throughout my 20s I was always taking my YFC kids out and being their sounding board when challenges were occurring in their lives. Today most of my "kids" are in their 40s with kids of their own. Now it's even more fun to be their peer as well as their Big Sister.

My time with Ray and Becca was priceless. I was blown away when they both went out of their way separately to bless ME while I was with them. Becca bought me coffee and lunch during the day we spent together, and Ray and his wife donated gas money to support my Adventure. Both times I felt like a proud parent watching them "take care of me" after all those years I took care of them when they were younger.

During the next leg of my journey the Lord gave me an unexpected gift. As I was traveling to speak at the CR in Wellsville, NY I had been asking the Lord to help me find my old YFC boss and mentor, Ralph, who lived in the area. I tried to locate him during the previous two weeks with no progress. Sadly, we had lost touch many years ago. I wanted to catch up with him while I was in Wellsville along with inviting him to hear my testimony at CR.

The day before I arrived in Wellsville, I took a chance and went online to whitepages.com. There were several people in the area, who had the same first and last name, so I choose the one I thought was him, left a voicemail, and hoped for the best. Three hours later I received a call from Ralph, surprised and thrilled I was in town after almost 30 years.

Ralph and his wife invited me to stay with them that evening, giving me even more time than I requested from the Lord to reconnect. Ralph also told our former YFC secretary, Barb, that I was in the area and she met us for lunch the next day. It was a wonderful YFC reunion! I love how the Lord gives us more than we can ask or imagine because of how much He loves us!

My testimony that evening at the Wellsville CR went well and, as always, it was wonderful getting to know my CR family and the CR leaders who let me stay at their home. I'm so glad the Lord prompted me to include my CR family as a part of this Adventure. The people I've met and the stories they've shared about the transformation they've experienced in their lives from extremely difficult situations and past emotional pain has been truly a wonder to behold.

Without all that baggage they are free to be who they are meant to be. And because their identity is grounded in Jesus, they have a deep joy and inner peace that impacts everyone they spend time with - who wouldn't want to be around that? :)

Yesterday I arrived at my Aunt and Uncle's home and today I had an opportunity to visit with my cousin. After that my Aunt and I stopped by to see my grandmother in her nursing home. She turned 91 recently, so I took a picture of the three of us and sent it to my mother so she could share in the moment even though she wasn't physically there.

I guess it's about time to wrap up this blog post. I have a few more kids to reconnect with as well as Ray & Becca's mom, so memory lane will continue over the next few weeks.

Let me leave you with a Psalm that seems to sum up my adventure so far. I hope it brings a smile to your face and an extra dose of confidence as you journey through whatever circumstances you are experiencing right now:

Psalm 16:5-11:

Lord, you alone are my portion and my cup; you make my lot secure.

The boundary lines have fallen for me in pleasant places; surely I have a delightful inheritance.

I will praise the Lord, who counsels me; even at night my heart instructs me.

I keep my eyes always on the Lord.

With him at my right hand, I will not be shaken.

Therefore my heart is glad and my tongue rejoices; my body also will rest secure, because you will not abandon me to the realm of the dead, nor will you let your faithful one see decay.

You make known to me the path of life; you will fill me with joy in your presence, with eternal pleasures at your right hand.

Chapter 9 - Divine Connections

Throughout the 50 years I've been on this earth, I've lived in seven states and moved close to 20 times (sometimes multiple moves in and out of a state!). Needless to say, countless numbers of people have come in and out of my life from the various communities where I've resided. Some of those people have become life-long friends while others have been part of my life for a season. And others have disappeared and then come back, picking up right where we left off as though no time had passed at all (I love that!).

The Lord has always opened doors to develop great friendships any place I've lived. Regardless of my many moves, I've always been proactive to maintain the relationships I care about most. Periodic catch up calls work well to reconnect even if it's only for 20-minutes during a busy day.

Looking back, several of those relationships have also been "divine connections" though I didn't know it when I met them and chose to maintain those relationships year after year. Future circumstances and many conversations later uncovered G-d's hand in setting up those relationships. Either He gave that person to me, or gave me to them, because He knew we would need to walk together during some truly hard seasons in life. Sometimes it was because the Lord wanted to do something bigger than both of us, and the timing of our connection was part of His plan.

One of those "divine connection" moments happened just a few days ago. As I was at my Aunt's house preparing for the next stop in my Adventure, the Lord prompted me to resend an email to Patty, a business woman I had been connecting with for years through my business. We have never met because she lives in Ohio. In 2010 I gave a virtual presentation to her women's networking group and we've stayed in touch ever since.

The Lord was preparing the way for His divine connection earlier this year unbeknownst to both of us when I reached out to say hello back in March. We had a 45-minute phone conversation trading stories about what the Lord was doing in each of our lives. I had no idea she had a deep relationship with the Lord and was even more surprised to learn she was wading deeply in the Holy Spirit pool of supernatural experiences that I aspired to experience myself. By the time I got off the call I knew she was going to be important in my spiritual development in some way. I made a mental note to follow up in a few months and continued on with my day.

In mid-July when I realized I was going through Ohio on my Adventure, the Lord prompted me to send an email to see if I could stop by to finally meet her in person. She's really good about responding to my emails, so when I didn't get a response I figured my email had gotten lost in cyberspace or that the Lord wanted to send me in another direction. I let it go and began my Adventure later that month.

When the Lord brought her to mind again at the beginning of August while at my Aunt's home, I couldn't find her phone number so I emailed her hoping she would receive it. The next morning as I was packing up to leave, my cell phone rang with a number I didn't recognize. It was Patty with an apology that she never got my original email followed by something like this: "It seems the Lord timed you're Adventure perfectly. I'm writing a book about finding one's calling, and your Adventure aligns with what I'm writing. You can absolutely stay with me a few days so we can talk more about what you're experiencing through your Adventure, and so we can finally get to know each other better." Only the Lord could've planned the timing of that!

Then the Lord did one better. It turned out that Patty teaches a class at CLU's School of the Spirit, a program aligned with the holy spirit training I was experiencing in my life. She invited me to attend her class while I was there to learn more about the Holy Spirit anointing I had been studying over the past year. AMAZING!! Once again, the Lord continues to bless me with spiritual growth opportunities because I am obediently trusting him day by day throughout my Adventure.

After that call I headed to Buffalo to see a friend named Amy. We walked around the revitalized waterfront, went to dinner, and then attended a praise and worship event. Amy is another one of my "divine connections." We met in 2009 and started to recognize G-d's hand in our friendship around three years later, and have been a blessing to each other ever since.

After Buffalo, NY I headed to Pat's home (Becca & Ray's mom) to speak at the CR in her area. Pat has always been a second mom to me ever since she and her family adopted me back in 1987. It had been several years since we had spoken on the phone and even longer since we'd seen each other in person. Because the CR meeting was scheduled for five days later, Pat and I had an extended amount of time to catch up and I finally had a chance to rest and leisurely go through the massive amounts of emails I received during my trip.

In any Adventure story there is always a protagonist (the leading character) and an antagonist (someone or something that interferes with what the leading character is trying to do). My recurring antagonist throughout this Adventure has been the lack of reliable cell service in the rural areas I've traveled through. I can't tell you the number of times I've had no bars or no 3G/4G connection for many, many miles.

My most amusing stories of dealing with this annoying antagonist have been just this last week. When I was heading to Pat's home the GPS sent me to a field in the middle of nowhere rather than her house. With no cell service I had no way to call her and no way to access Google Maps on my phone to see where I was. All I saw around me were farms and fields. I asked the Lord for help and kept driving for about eight miles until I saw a business with cars in front of it.

I went inside, told them I was from Georgia (I figured that would give me immediate sympathy since I was in rural NY) and that my GPS wasn't playing nice. I asked if I could use their phone to call Pat to find out if there was another address I could use. The young woman in the front was happy to help, but the lady in the back was eyeing me up and down with a noticeably uneasy demeanor as though I was going to place a long-distance call to Europe on their dime.

I called Pat and told her about my dilemma. She apologized because GPS has done that before to other visitors. After receiving directions from where she thought I was, I left and monitored my phone for cell service since Pat didn't have a car to come find me if I got lost again. Ten miles later I still had no bars and I hoped I was going in the right direction. Then just around a bend I saw a sign with the name of her town and started to breathe easier.

My cell service challenges continued the next day when I drove North seven miles, South six miles, West five miles, and then East for eight more miles. NO SIGNAL, ANYWHERE! I was still committed to not let anything steal my joy, so when I saw a Verizon store I chuckled. I don't have Verizon service, but I know they have the best cell service coverage hands down of all the carriers. I figured it wouldn't hurt to take a chance to see if they could help.

I walked into the store and knew I was in Verizon territory because all the sales people were dressed very professionally. One eager 20-something young man walked up to me and asked how he could help. I told him I had been driving around for 30-minutes trying to find cell service for my provider and couldn't find any, and did he know where I could find it?

Another sales person walked over and laughed good-naturedly saying, "oh…about 20-30 miles from here." I shook my head and sighed. The younger salesperson immediately asked, "You want to switch to Verizon?" Can't blame him for trying, right? :)

I smiled and laughed at his quick sales pitch explaining that I was visiting from Atlanta where my coverage was great, and that even though Verizon was superior, I was not willing to pay Verizon prices for just a month or two of service before heading home. They understood and graciously offered to let me borrow their wi-fi to get onto my carrier's website to check the coverage map for the nearest service area.

After looking for a few minutes at the coverage map I saw a wide zone of service to the west and asked them where it was. It turned out to be a town about 12 miles away on a road I had not traveled in my earlier cell zone quest. I thanked them, headed in that direction and seven miles later my phone began dinging many times with text messages and voicemails.

I pulled off the road to check them and lost the signal again. I must've driven through a very small section of coverage with just enough time to download that stuff to my phone. I kept heading west to the town that had service coverage and three miles later my phone started dinging again. When I found a safe place to pull over, I saw 3G next to my cell bars and smiled. Finally! 10 miles from where I was staying, I had finally found reliable cell service. I pulled out my GPS and marked that location so I could stop there every day during my stay.

The Lord provided another troubleshooting option as well through a wi-fi app which allows a cell phone to make calls over a wi-fi service. I had no idea how to set that up, so I started researching it until the Lord prompted me to check with Vonage (the wi-fi company I use for my business phone #). They had a wi-fi app I could download, and after a few challenges of trying to set it up I was able to make outgoing calls from Pat's home and continued to drive a few miles to receive and send texts.

This weekend I'm heading to the home of another one of my YFC kids followed by a visit to Patty's home in Ohio next week. To wrap up this blog post, here's one of my favorite verses and a great theme for my Adventure: "Have I not commanded you? Be strong and courageous. Do not be terrified; do not be discouraged, for the LORD your God will be with you wherever you go" (Joshua 1:9).

I remain strong and courageous in the Lord and am doing my best to not fear or be discouraged when obstacles appear - because I know the Lord is with me wherever I go!

Have a great rest of your day!! :) ~Kris

Chapter 10 - Your Story Can Save A Life

<u>*August 11*</u>

Hi all! Ike Ikokwu has been following my G-d Adventure Sabbatical blog series since I left in July. When I asked him if my story would be a good fit for his #YourStoryCanSaveALifeChallenge series, he absolutely agreed. We all have stories that can save someone else's life.

Here's Ike's explanation for his video series: "The #YourStoryCanSaveALifeChallenge series on social media is an effort to share stories of triumph over adversity that can help curb the tide of suicide globally. I hope you'll join the movement by sharing your story on social media using the hashtag, #YourStoryCanSaveALifeChallenge. Then ask a few of your contacts to do the same by tagging them. Together, maybe we can save a life!"

Thanks for watching my interview with Ike! If you want to connect with Ike, here's his Facebook page (send him a message that you saw my interview with him so he has a frame of reference for the friend request):

https://www.facebook.com/ike.ikokwu .

Have a wonderful rest of your week! ~Kris

**To access Video link, go to:
http://BeginToShift.com/crazy-blessing-videos**

Chapter 11 - Look At Her Necklace

August 12

I left on 8/11/Sat morning from Pat's western NY home to head back to Pennsylvania to visit Ricky, one of my Indiana Youth For Christ (YFC) kids. Ricky and his family were going to be at a work picnic the day I arrived. If I got into town early, they suggested hanging out at a Starbucks about 15-minutes from their home. I knew I would get there in the afternoon, so I plugged the address into the GPS and left NY to head in that direction.

After being on the road for over three hours I got off the highway and drove through beautiful country roads with fields and rolling hills for miles. As I rounded a bend in the road, I suddenly saw a town with several bridges and a large river running through it. The view was such a dramatic change of scenery from where I had been driving, and so very beautiful, that I had to stop and walk around.

As I crossed the bridge, I saw that I was entering Monaca, PA. On the other side of the bridge I saw a road heading down to the river, and a minute later I saw another road next to the river near a walking path. After parking the car, I marveled at the oasis of beauty I found.

The next part of my story is going to blow your mind. I had just walked down the path, fully enjoying the scenery, and finished taking all the pictures I wanted. On my way back to the car, I passed a Castle for the second time and wondered what historical significance it represented. When I saw two guys walking down the path towards me, I interrupted their conversation to ask if they had any information about the Castle. They smiled, said they didn't know anything, and suggested I ask someone that lived in the area.

Then suddenly the younger guy's eyes got completely wide and he exclaimed, "Look at her necklace! Shabbat Shalom!" The older guy then looks at my necklace, also surprised, and joyfully repeats, "Shabbat Shalom." My necklace is called a Messianic Seal. It has the Jewish Menorah on the top and the Christian Fish *symbol on the bottom; merged together in the middle is the Star of David. It symbolizes an affiliation with a Messianic Jewish-Gentile congregation.*

Both guys start asking me questions about whether I live in Monaca and said that their Messianic Congregation was having a picnic and studying Torah near the playground. After telling them I'm from a Messianic congregation in Georgia and on a G-d Adventure, they encouraged me to stop by their group and say hello. I sensed the Lord all over this divine encounter, so of course I headed over to the playground.

The group was praying when I got close, so I stood off to the side and waited for them to finish. When they opened their eyes, I said, "Shabbat Shalom" and told them about my encounter with the two guys by the castle who said I should stop by. Everyone immediately welcomed me and started introducing themselves (there were about seven people total).

It turns out they are the only Messianic Congregation in the area. Because they are still a small group, they usually rent space for Shabbat Services and Torah Study in a building in another town. However, because of the beautiful weather, they had chosen this outdoor location today.

My G-d Adventure intrigued them, so I gave them the abbreviated version of the Lord asking me to pack up my stuff and go just like Abraham. I then handed them a business card with my website and told them they could read all about it on my blog.

We chatted for a few minutes, then they asked if they could pray for me and my journey to which I said "absolutely!" What a lovely group of people and a truly wonderful prayer for journey mercies, protection and provision. I then prayed for them, said my good-byes, and headed off to grab dinner while I was waiting for Ricky and his family to arrive home.

Amazing! Only G-d could've coordinated that divine encounter which never would've happened if I had not taken the time to drive down to the river to walk around, and if I had simply passed by the guys without asking about the Castle.

As I sit here munching on my dinner and writing this blog entry, I am continually astonished at how the Lord keeps setting up "G-d moments" to show me His presence throughout my journey.

I'll be staying with Ricky and his wife for a day or so, and then heading off to see Patty. After that I have a few other planned stops, but no timeline. Based on what's been happening over the last two weeks, I expect I'll have several unscheduled stops as well!

Have a fantastic rest of your day. Blessings and Favor to you! ~Kris

Chapter 12 - Walk By Faith, Not By Sight

<u>*August 19*</u>

As of today, I have been on the road for almost a month. My visit with Ricky, his wife Julie, and their family went great. On Sunday we took a drive to McConnell Mill Park and Hell's Hallow Falls. The water levels were really low, so the falls weren't as spectacular as usual, but the scenery around it was fantastic. While we were there, I shared snippets about my G-d Adventure. I also told Julie about my Youth For Christ days in Tipton, IN and how the Lord led me to "adopt" Ricky and a few other kids in the area.

After we got back to their house and began sharing our individual pictures from the day, Julie was amazed at one of the shots she captured. The first two of Ricky and I on the rocks were nice, but the third shot became another G-d moment. Two light beams appeared out of nowhere which landed on me and on Ricky. I'm sure it was G-d smiling on both of us. :)

The next day while Ricky was at work I began contemplating and praying about whether to head West to Washington state or South to Florida after my stop in Indiana to speak at a CR and visit with my Indiana YFC kids. I was still not clear about the direction the Lord wanted to take me, so I decided to map out the CRs every 250 miles by meeting day in order to hit one a day from Indiana to North Dakota (just over 1000 miles total). I contacted the CR Leaders for all those groups and figured if enough of them said "yes," that would be my answer.

The next day I headed to OH to see Patty. When I arrived at her home, we hugged each other joyfully and laughed because it was the first time we've met in person after eight years of connecting via phone and email. We both had such a great visit that we were sad I had to leave after a few days. But we both knew the Lord had more Adventures in store for me as I kept moving forward from place to place.

During my visit, the Lord provided many divine conversations, G-d moments and even unexpected provision, including this story: Before I left Ricky's home, I knew my car needed an oil change and I figured I could stop and get it done in OH or IN at a local oil shop. While I was at Patty's I reminded the Lord that I needed the oil changed and asked Him to coordinate the money and the place to get it done.

A few hours later, without knowing anything about my prayer, Patty said to me, "Would you like my husband to change your oil before you go?" I chuckled, silently thanked the Lord, and said yes! I already had four quarts of oil in the trunk because the engine has been leaking oil for about two years. All her husband needed to do was buy a filter and change it. That's Jehovah Jireh in action!

The Lord also provided additional insight about which direction to head (West or South) after Indiana when I received a call from the North Dakota CR saying they would love to have me give my testimony and would be happy to find someone to host me for a night. I was still apprehensive about heading West because their CR was 1000 miles from Indiana. I didn't have any other CR scheduled in between to break up the drive, so I told the leader to give me a few days to pray about it. I went to bed with a sneaky suspicion that the Lord purposely had the farthest CR call me as a faith test to see if I would keep following His lead in this Adventure, trusting He would provide for housing in between.

Besides housing, I was also concerned about my unreliable cell reception. I didn't want to get stuck on a mountain range in the middle of nowhere without cell reception if something happened. The Lord began addressing that concern quickly.

The moment I arrived at Patty's house my phone started having charging issues, which meant that I may have to get another phone regardless of what service I had. That, of course, reminded me of my previous Verizon conversation from when I was staying with Pat. Verizon mentioned I could temporarily switch cell service, without a contract, if someone with Verizon service would add me to their family plan on a monthly basis. I could cancel the service whenever I wanted to without a penalty (all I had to do was pay for the phone).

I sensed the Lord was causing my phone issues to show me that the inconvenience of having to switch providers and phones was simply that…an inconvenience. I also recognized I was having another "idol" moment (remember chapter 3?) as I started to complain about all the hours it would take to set up the apps correctly on the new phone.

I asked the Lord to forgive me, then called my Dad to see if I could jump onto his plan. He agreed and Patty dropped me at a Verizon store later that day while she ran an errand. As it turned out that solution was perfect for my dilemma, but my Dad was not available to do the transfer when they called him for authorization.

As I waited for Patty to pick me up, I felt much more confident about going West. I called Rick (the consultant I work for part-time) and left a voicemail alerting him of the possibility of heading West and that my work availability may be sporadic over the next week or so. When I hung up the phone, I was still not fully committed to going to West. However, I told the Lord I would continue to walk by faith and not by sight (2 Cor 5:7) because He invited me on this Adventure and because I knew He was fully capable of taking care of me between IN and ND.

When I got up the next morning there was a short text from Rick: "Thanks for your call. Going Left, eh? Exciting!" As I read it, I thought it was strange that he used the word "Left" instead of West, but I completely understood his message and laughed. The word "Left" stayed with me all day and I knew it was the Lord trying to tell me something.

The next evening when I arrived in Indiana, I received an email with an MP3 attached to it from two of my trusted godly friends who had gotten together to prophetically pray for my journey. Within 30 seconds of listening to the prayer, one of them says, "I see the words 'Go Left.' I'm not sure if that means go left on the road you are on right now or go left of Indiana. You'll have to pray about that."

I laughed out loud because I knew in that moment that Rick's "left" comment and my friend's "left" message was the Lord's way of easing any doubts I had about saying "yes" to the North Dakota CR.

As I prepare to head West, I do not have any scheduled stops along the 1000-mile trip from IN to ND. I'm hoping that changes soon and am surrendering the outcome to the Lord. I know He's got me in His capable hands. Though to be honest, I am a bit anxious about just going "Left" and seeing what happens. However, I have a feeling the deeper level of faith that will be required on this part of my journey is all part of the Lord's plan.

This closing verse is as much for me as it is for anyone reading this post: "Trusting is being confident of what we hope for, convinced about things we do not see. It was for this that Scripture attested the merit of the people of old…..And without trusting, it is impossible to be well pleasing to God, because whoever approaches him must trust that he does exist and that he becomes a Rewarder to those who seek him out." (Hebrews 11:1, 2 and 6).

Have a great rest of your day! I'll write another blog as soon as I have time to do so.

BLESSINGS to you! ~Kris

Chapter 13 - Don't Judge A Book By Its Cover

<u>*August 23*</u>

It's almost 4 AM right now. I can't seem to shut my brain off, so I decided to get out of bed and write this blog entry. "Amazing" doesn't even come close to describing the last seven days of my journey. There's too much to tell so I'll be dividing those stories between this blog post and the next one.

If you'll recall in my previous post, I mentioned I left OH on 8/16/Thu and headed to Hartford City, IN to speak at a CR group. As always, the Lord set up the evening for the right people to be in the room, including two significant divine connections. As I begin that story, I want to assure you I was given permission to share it.

When I arrived in Hartford City, I was tired from the long drive and pulled over at the local high school to take a nap in their parking lot. About 45-minutes later I headed over to the CR group and introduced myself to the Leader named Larry. We chatted for a bit and then a woman named Belinda walked up to join us. Larry had to get some stuff done so he left me with Belinda and walked away.

Belinda immediately started asking me a series of questions, but it felt more like an interrogation than a conversation. I was unsure of the reason for her intense line of questioning, but I joyfully told her my story and provided answers to everything she asked. When Larry walked back over to us, Belinda made a quick exit which surprised me as well. I asked Larry if Belinda was on the CR leadership team. Larry informed me that she was his wife which made me even more curious about her approach to our conversation. However, I figured the Lord knew her heart and would work it all out.

During the CR program I gave my testimony, and that was an interesting experience as well. I've been public speaking since I was 17 and I know how to keep track of the audience's reactions while I'm moving through my material. Most of the time people laugh in the same places or sit quietly with the tension of anticipation on their faces waiting to find out how my testimony ends.

This time, however, my experience was completely different. The lighting on the stage was so bright I couldn't see the audience well. During the funny parts of my story no one laughed and the body language I could see from the stage seemed more passive than actively engaged in what I was saying. By the time I finished with my testimony I had no idea how I had been received other than the typical "end clap" from everyone in the room. I was a bit worried as I left the pulpit, but I knew the Lord wanted me there and trusted the right people heard what He wanted them to hear.

I sat back down and waited for the program to finish. Then Larry asked Belinda to say the closing prayer. She walked up to the front, and suddenly turned around asking me to come up front so they could pray for me. A pang of concern flowed through me in response to my experience with her earlier. I wondered what to expect and then in a split second everything changed.

Belinda walked down the aisle to meet me, grabbed my hand, pulled me to the front of the church, and began praying for me in a powerful way full of blessings and thankfulness for my testimony. It was such a radical transformation from earlier that I knew the Lord set up our previous "interrogation" in order to speak to her heart about whatever was going on in her life. Afterwards other people in the audience also stopped by to thank me for my testimony. Later as I was leaving, Larry and Belinda asked to meet me for coffee the next morning before I headed out to Tipton, IN to see my kids, and I was happy to do so.

We met at a local restaurant at 9 AM and our breakfast conversation became a confessional over coffee. Belinda revealed that she had been struggling with Larry's decision to let me speak at their CR group without doing any research on me. Earlier that week when he informed her about it, she asked him multiple questions about me including what I had been in recovery for, why was I traveling across the states, and did anyone else have any experience with me?

Larry said he had no idea, and it didn't matter because he knew for sure the Lord wanted him to say yes. He was completely at ease about my invitation. Belinda, however, was not at all at peace, and certainly not satisfied nor happy with his answer. Out of frustration with him, she decided to get those answers the moment I arrived which was the reason for the instant interrogation when Larry walked away from us.

As Belinda continued to share the back story with me, she laughed and said the entire time she was asking me questions she didn't understand why I was being so darn nice to her. By the end of that conversation she still wasn't at peace with my arrival which is why she bolted quickly when Larry walked back over.

She remained uneasy about me right until I began my testimony. Then the Lord started speaking to her about how she approached me, revealing that it mirrored the struggles she was experiencing in many areas of her life. By the end of my testimony she had a deep respect for me and truly accepted the Lord's divine appointment at their CR group.

Throughout her coffee confessional I sensed she had the same type of personality as me, so I looked her straight in the eye, lovingly smiled, laughed, and acknowledged my confusion at her interrogation. I told her that I chose to ignore her behavior and remain joyful and transparent while answering her questions despite it because I knew my arrival in Hartford City was ordained by the Lord; and because I knew her reaction to me was not my responsibility.

Belinda laughed at my directness and apologized for her poor reaction to me (I love how people who are serious about their recovery "own" their stuff!). Then she asked my forgiveness for how she treated me. She said that the Lord used me to teach her not to judge a book by its cover which made me laugh out loud again. The rest of the breakfast we traded stories and continued laughing a lot. By the time I left I knew I had made a new friend and that we would most likely stay in touch for years to come.

I left for Tipton, IN after that to find one of my Youth For Christ (YFC) kids. I had lost touch with Jason several years back and had been trying to find him online for the last two years. Several people I knew from Tipton were also checking their network, but no one could locate him. It turned out that while I was at the Hartford City CR, the Lord prompted me to share my "lost kid" dilemma with a couple in the audience, and they turned out to be another divine connection. The husband knew someone who could help me and gave me that person's phone number.

The morning Larry, Belinda and I had breakfast, we contacted that person and he was able to give me several pieces of information, including Jason's last known address. Once again, the Lord blessed me through my obedience in following His lead as I gave my testimony to CR groups across the country!

On my way to Tipton, I headed over to the town of Jason's last known address, found the house, and knocked on the door. There was no response, but I heard a dog barking inside. I knocked again and still no response. I taped a note to the front door with my phone number asking whoever lived there to call me.

Upon arriving in Tipton, I did more research to try and find Jason with no success. As I headed back to my car to find a place for lunch, I noticed I had voicemail from a local number: "Yorka! Yorka! You should've knocked harder. I was sleeping. Give me a call back."

You should've seen my face. I was overwhelmed at the Lord's kindness to have so quickly located my "kid" after years of trying to find him. It was a joy to hear Jason's voice. I called him and drove back to his house. When he answered the door, I gave him a big hug, took a picture of us, and sent it to Melisa and Ricky (my other kids) who had been helping me try to find him. Melisa and her husband, Scott, met up with Jason and I later. The four of us had a great reunion over dinner that night.

If you are wondering about the "Yorka" name, it goes back to 1990 when I arrived in Tipton, IN as the YFC for Tipton County. I grew up north of New York City and spent a lot of time in the city visiting family or working with my Dad in his advertising agency during summer breaks. Years later when the Lord sent me to Indiana after graduating college to work with YFC, I was having quite a bit of culture shock as I settled into their very rural town. All my YFC kids used to tease me about my former big city life, which sparked the nickname "Yorka." In response to their teasing, I lovingly started calling Melisa "Hoosier," and we've been using those nicknames ever since.

Over the next few days I revisited memory after memory as I stopped at restaurants and other places I used to hang out with my YFC kids. Then suddenly the Tipton visit ended abruptly, and the Lord arranged a divine layover leading me back to Larry and Belinda's home for several days. I'll share that story in the next blog post.

Until then, here are a few verses which reflect this part of my Adventure. They are great reminders to not judge a book by its cover:

> *"But the Lord said to Samuel, 'Do not look at his appearance or at the height of his stature….for God sees not as man sees, for man looks at the outward appearance, but the Lord looks at the heart" (1 Samuel 16:7)*

> *"I, the Lord, search the heart and examine the mind, to reward each person according to their conduct, according to what their deeds deserve" (Jeremiah 17:10)*

> *"O Lord, You have searched me and known me" (Psalm 139:1)*

> *"All a person's ways seem pure to them, but motives are weighed by the Lord" (Proverbs 16:2)*

The last few days I've been planning my trip West and so far the Lord has opened up a CR in Iowa and two in North Dakota to break up the 1000 mile ride. I've got several more on my radar after that as I head to the coast of Washington state and then I'll start contacting other CRs from there to Los Angeles, CA.

The adventure has become significantly longer than I expected, and I still don't know when it will come to an end. Regardless of the unknown timeline, I continue to live "one day at a time" trusting the Lord will provide money to pay the bills and provide housing or hotels along my route.

Enjoy the rest of your week, everyone!

:) ~Kris

Chapter 14 - Divine Layover

You know the old saying, _"Man Plans, God Laughs"?_ I had a dose of that last week. One thing I know about the Lord is that He's never laughing maliciously. It's always joyfully because His plans are so much better than ours.

In my last post I left you hanging about my visit in Tipton, IN ending abruptly on 8/21/Tues. The weekend before, I spent quite a bit of time mapping out my desired stops and potential CR groups within those areas because I needed to be at the CR in Sioux Center, Iowa on 8/27/Mon which was 700+ miles from Tipton.

Driving over 11 hours in a day would be exhausting, and I knew I would not be at my best to be fully present for the CR program in addition to giving my testimony that night. If knew if I could find a few CRs between Thursday and Monday, that would break up the long trek to Iowa.

I followed my typical routine of emailing the CR leaders in each of the cities where I wanted to stop, wait a day, and then follow up my email with a phone call. None of the leaders answered their phones when I called. I left voicemails hoping one of them would say yes.

Meanwhile during my Tipton visit, Belinda (the CR leader's wife from the previous blog post) called me on 8/20/Mon to follow up about two other CRs in their area which they felt could benefit from my testimony. Larry had contacted them the previous Friday, but neither group had responded. Belinda then shared how she felt the Lord wanting her to open up her home to me so I could be available to other ladies in the community as the Lord led her to make those connections.

She laughed and said that she argued a bit with the Lord at first because she and her husband had bought their house as a fixer-upper. It had been torn up and in various stages of demolition ever since. She had never allowed anyone to come into her home, let alone a woman she had just met, but the Lord really laid it on her heart to extend the invitation.

The moment she offered me the opportunity to stay at her home, I knew the Lord was getting ready to set her table for a variety of divine conversations. I eagerly said yes knowing that I could leave within a day if the CRs I contacted between Indiana and Iowa called me back to request my testimony at their group. I then felt the Lord prompt me to offer a leadership and coaching skills training workshop at no cost for whomever she wanted to invite. She eagerly said yes and said she would see what she could coordinate.

I arrived at Belinda and Larry's home the next day. Within seconds Belinda and I started joking around like we had known each other for years. Whenever that happens, I know I've made a friend for life.

Later that evening we took a drive to the Double R Ranch to talk to the woman hosting a retreat Belinda was supposed to attend that weekend. She had never visited the ranch before and didn't think she would be able to go because I might be staying through the weekend if no CRs opened up before I had to leave on Monday for Iowa.

We arrived at the ranch a few minutes later and both our jaws dropped as we drove up the long driveway to the main house. The owners had rebuilt their barn into a B&B Retreat Home, and it looked like something right out of a movie: horses in the field, a huge garden on one side, acres and acres of land, and a separate guest house for more private events.

Beth, the owner, came out to meet us and gave Belinda a big hug because they've known each other for years. Belinda then introduced Beth to me. For the next few minutes Belinda and Beth spent time catching up, and then Beth gave us a tour of the main house.

From one room to the next it went from amazing to more amazing. Each room had a different cowboy theme and included materials from the original barn which they had salvaged during the renovation. Beth gave us the backstory of how they came to a decision to change their home from a farm environment to a B&B Retreat Home, along with the renovation challenges they faced as the barn was transformed from floor to ceiling. By the end of the tour Belinda and I were in awe and couldn't stop raving about it.

Belinda shared with Beth that she wasn't sure she could make the women's retreat that weekend because of my arrival at their home, and then shared my G-d Adventure Sabbatical story along with how Belinda and I met. Beth had a feeling the Lord had coordinated the retreat to be at the same time as my visit, so she said she would do a final guest check to see if there was room for one more.

As we left, I had a suspicion that the CRs I had tried so hard to land between Thursday and Monday would not be available - and I was right. The Lord definitely had a "divine layover" planned for me to join that women's retreat on Friday and Saturday when Beth called the next day saying she had one more space available and would love to have me attend. To prepare for the retreat Beth asked us to bring shoes that could get dirty to walk through the prayer labyrinth she created a few years ago in one of her lower fields.

I mentioned to Belinda that I only packed what I needed for my Adventure which did not include old shoes. I also didn't have a jacket because I left GA in July with only a sweater (I had not factored in the cooler weather at night throughout the northern U.S). Belinda said not to worry about it. She was sure they could find something for me to borrow and showed me a selection of jackets to choose from. The one I selected was one she didn't wear anymore so it became her gift to me.

The next day Belinda had to run a few errands. She returned later and handed me a bag full of goodies. On her way home, she stopped at the dollar store to pick something up for her house and noticed a bunch of sneakers on a shelf along with several audio books and CDs further down the row. After looking through them she selected three CD sets she thought I might like for my journey to Iowa and grabbed a pair of sneakers and some walk around socks for the retreat so I didn't have to get mine dirty. How thoughtful!!! I thanked her profusely and smiled brightly.

As I expected, the divine conversations at Belinda's home started happening later that evening and continued throughout my visit, with multiple opportunities to utilize my coaching and training skills as hearts were shared on a variety of topics over the next few days. It was such a joy to be of service to the Lord and to a variety of ladies while I was there.

On Friday Belinda and I left for the retreat. Eleven ladies attended, and for the most part they already knew each other well. As I got to know them, I quickly saw that they each loved the Lord deeply. The retreat was remarkable in more ways than I can describe. At one point I was so overcome with emotion that I had to walk away from the group to a quiet spot staring out the window with tears streaming down my face because of the joy and thankfulness I was feeling for the Lord to have arranged the entire retreat as a gift to me during my journey.

The theme for the retreat was a study on Esther using a mixture of Beth Moore videos and Tony Evans study materials, followed by small group discussions, other events, and of course FOOD! Beth's kitchen was huge and did not lack for any savory treats or healthy options along with coffee and tea galore! Beth's gift of hospitality shined brightly all weekend and her home became my home the entire time I was there.

The most memorable moment for me during the weekend was the Prayer Labyrinth. Saturday morning there was a serious storm and it poured hard for several hours. By mid-afternoon the sun came out and it was a beautiful day. Because Indiana is mostly flat, flooding happens easily. Beth had a feeling that the field would be too wet for the group to enjoy walking around the Labyrinth and suggested a few other activities. After spending the morning studying Esther, we were all ready for a break and decided to walk down to the field anyway to at least see the Labyrinth from a distance.

As Beth expected, the entire area was flooded. Some of the ladies were feeling child-like, so they took off their shoes and began to walk barefoot through the water towards the location of the Labyrinth. Thanks to Belinda's gift of sneakers and socks, I kept mine on and followed *them (the water was only about 8 inches deep). The ladies were laughing as they playfully splashed their feet up and down remembering childhood moments.*

As I continued with them to the Labyrinth, in my mind I expected it to be an intimidating maze of tall bushes (the kind you can't see over and can easily get lost in) similar to the huge mazes at European castles.

Beth's version was so drastically different from what my mind had envisioned that when I rounded the corner and saw the ladies walking around a short grassy area in a maze-like fashion, I laughed out loud with glee. The Labyrinth was a mowed-out section of grass about a foot high. That area was flooded too, but I couldn't resist the experience. Since my feet and legs were already soaked, I walked the Labyrinth with the other ladies silently praising the Lord for yet another moment of joy He had given me.

We all started the Labyrinth at different times and quietly waited for the last person to meet us in the middle. As the last person arrived, we shared a group hug and I took a picture to memorialize the experience.

The walk back through the water was just as fun, and it gave me an opportunity to talk to one of the ladies I had not yet spent any time with. As we were passing the horse field I stopped and made a clicking sound. The horses responded as I hoped by walking over to the fence so I could pet them.

The rest of the retreat was amazing too, especially the impromptu praise song from Belinda using Hillsong's "New Wine" acoustic version during our journaling time. When Belinda started to sing, I was blown away by the quality of her voice. If I did not know she was playing the song in the background on a speaker, I would've sworn Hillsong had been in the room.

Journaling has been a common routine for me since 2012, and I've used several journaling methods. It wasn't until my visit with Patty in Ohio that I came to understand the power of interactive journaling with the Lord until she gave me a book called, *"4 Keys to Hearing God's Voice"*[4] by Mark and Patti Virkler. During my stay with Patty, I read through part of his book and practiced journaling in the way Virkler suggested. What a transformational difference in my ability to hear from the Lord even more clearly than I had in the past. WOW!

The way it works is this: You start out by envisioning yourself with Jesus in a special place. Once you see yourself with Jesus, ask Him a question or share what's on your heart, writing down whatever you say to the Lord in your journal. You then silently listen for His answer. As you sense the Lord responding, you just write it down in your journal without editing the content or stopping to think about how rational it sounds because doing so will interrupt the flow of the Holy Spirit.

Once you feel the Lord is done speaking, you can continue to repeat the cycle over and over until your conversation is finished. Only when you are done do you meditate on what you wrote down and prayerfully test it (1 John 4:1) to make sure the message you received is from the Lord and not from your rational mind or from the enemy.

As all the ladies began to journal, the Holy Spirit was powerfully present in the room. Below is my journal conversation with the Lord. When I finished, I sensed the conversation was not only for me, but also for the whole group. I ended up sharing the journal entry with the other ladies later that day and several of the women thanked me for doing so.

I'll bet as you read it, it will be applicable for you too because the Lord knew I would be blogging about this and He does not waste any opportunity to encourage all His kids! (Men – this is relevant for you too. Just replace the words daughter with son, she/her with he/his, or woman with man).

---

[4] Virkler, Mark & Patti. <u>4 Keys to Hearing God's Voice</u>, Shippensburg, PA: Destiny Image Publishers Inc, 2010.

(Kris' thoughts)

Lord, as I sit here among all these amazing women, I am awed at how much You love me to set up this entire Indiana trip as a Divine Layover so I could meet Belinda, have a coffee confessional with her, meet Beth, and then be invited to this incredible retreat environment surrounded by other women who love You as much, or even more than I do.

There is nothing like a woman sold out to you! She will knock down walls, risk bullets, and step off cliffs for You because she knows that she knows who Her Daddy is, and that He would never forsake her in any situation! That sold out woman is secure in her identity in You and will trust You even in life or death situations. She is a holy woman to be reckoned with in any situation. Nothing is too hard for her to handle because YOU are flowing through her.

I declare each woman here IS that woman - even if she doesn't know it yet! I declare a revolutionary transformation is occurring deep into every woman's DNA; that her soul and Your spirit are intersecting in such a profound way that she will now have the ability within seconds to tap into Your holy fire full of unlimited resources to receive exactly what she needs - the moment she needs it - from this point forward to address and overcome any personal or professional challenge she is currently facing.

I decree a holy anointing over every woman here, and that Your light will shine through them brightly, and that people they've been praying for will begin to soften and draw closer to them to receive what You have for their lives. May radical peace and joy show up in their lives in amazing ways from this day forth until You bring them home to experience it forever.

****

I paused a minute as I was listening to the music and asked the Lord if He wanted to share anything with me. This is what flowed from my spirit:

(Jesus' Reply)

Beloved daughters - not only will you receive that, I will give you more than you can ask or imagine because my love for you stretches as far as the East is from the West, and measures more than the number of stars in the sky. The next time you doubt that, just look up and see me winking at you [in my mind I saw the stars in the heaven "winking" on and off and Jesus smiling bright with a twinkle in His eye].

The phrase "what doesn't kill me makes me stronger" means more than you think. It's not just about surviving a situation. It's about stepping into your fullness of power and impact through me. Trust I cried with you in your pain, and with every tear you shed I used it to carve out a path for you to walk into your amazing future…even though it didn't feel like it at the time.

Don't ever forget you are my beautiful Bride destined for greatness, and nothing will ever make me love you any less. Your past will not hold hostage your future!! With me you are free to be yourself and enjoy life. And I, as your husband, will guide you and give you what you need every step of the way!

****

I certainly needed to hear what the Lord shared when I wrote it. I hope you benefited from it as well!

Beth's husband came home as we were finishing the retreat, so I asked him to take a picture for my blog. Another woman handed him her camera as well. After the two pictures were taken, I laughed when I compared them. The other woman's picture was a beautiful shot of everyone with no distortions of any kind and, of course, my camera took a G-d Shot: light cascading from the windows over all of us as though the Holy Spirit had come down to rest in our presence. LOVED THAT!!

As I finish up this blog, I am in North Dakota preparing to leave for my second CR visit in western ND before continuing West towards Washington. The Lord has still not given me any information about my stops between ND and WA. After tomorrow, I am "flying blind."

I suspected the Lord was going to withhold information for longer periods of time during this leg of my Adventure to train me to reach a new level of faith with Him. After all, the purpose of this journey is to set me up for whatever career or ministry He has for me next. So, am I worried? I think a better question is "Am I human?"

Of course, human worry shows up whenever uncertainty appears! But thanks to Celebrate Recovery I have truly learned how to live one day at a time. Anytime anxiety crosses my mind about gas money, the 1400+ mile drive between ND and WA, and where I will be sleeping each night, I hand my worries back over to the Lord. After all, He's gotten me this far!

My new motto is something I heard from the CR I spoke at in Iowa. One of the women mentioned this: "I must decide to trust G-d or I Don't. It's that simple." It really is that simple! So I choose to trust the Lord, and lay my worries down, replacing worry with faith that He will provide exactly what I need during this unknown section of my journey…especially because He invited me on this adventure! :)

"Be on your guard; stand firm in the faith; be courageous; be strong. Do everything in love." (1 Cor 16:13-14).

Enjoy the rest of your day, everyone! ~Kris

PS - If you want to stay at the Double R Ranch or book a retreat there, you can do so by looking for the ranch on GlampingHub.com in Hartford City, IN. Tell Beth I said hello when you book the reservation!

Chapter 15 - Radical Obedience

When I left Indiana and began heading West towards Washington, it was at that moment I truly began the "radical obedience" part of my Adventure. Up until that point I had been on familiar ground because no matter where I had traveled previously, Atlanta could be reached within 1000 miles from any direction. I also had family and friends scattered throughout the area. Essentially, I was in a "safe" zone which was why I knew I was struggling with the decision to go West or South after I finished my Indiana visit.

Leaving for the Adventure in July was a step into radical obedience, but for some reason it felt even more radical to drive out of my safety zone and head 2000 more miles across the country without knowing a soul in between Indiana and the coast of Washington.

Before I committed to heading West, I spent a lot of time reflecting on everything that had happened during the Adventure and all the moments where the Lord had showed up and showed off. My mind was still astonished at all the divine moments of provision and connections which had occurred in the last 30 days. The Adventure had been a series of blind faith decisions along with annoying challenges, and yet I didn't regret any of it. It was as if my life had become a movie in motion and I was in the audience with everyone else wondering what would happen next.

I processed through all my concerns about the next 2000 miles, followed by the 5000 miles that would follow to return to Atlanta. In my mind I had two scales: the "what if" scale of all the things that could go wrong and the "regret" scale of what I would miss if I didn't take the leap of faith and just go forward.

Regret always weighs heavier on my mind than any potential problems that could occur, which ultimately made it easier to make a decision. Even before Rick texted me with the word "left" and before I had received the email with the prophetic prayer confirming "left," I was already 80% at peace with going West. Those confirmations simply helped me cross the line to say yes more quickly than I would have otherwise.

As I continue to write this book, I am so thankful I did say YES to the Lord, and you'll see why as you read through the rest of the blog entries which are full of incredible G-d stories and lots of lessons I learned along the way.

There is no such thing as a boring life when you choose radical obedience. The experience of living that type of life is abundantly more valuable than you can imagine. All that's required is a "yes" and "amen" (2 Corinthians 1:20) to receive the promises that come from choosing to be radically obedient to the Lord's will for your life.

Earlier in the chapter titled "Acts Is A Lifestyle & Mindset," I stated that we were never meant to live normal lives. Normal is a world standard. G-d's standard is very different. The Lord is in the business of Kingdom impact to bring as many people into the family of Believers before Jesus returns to the Earth to bring us all home (Revelation 19).

Kingdom impact doesn't just happen. The Lord wants us to partner with Him in His work on Earth. The Bible is full of stories where the Lord asks a variety of men and women to partner with Him to achieve His desired outcome. Each one of those men and women opted for radical obedience to the Lord regardless of the pain and suffering they could experience along the way.

Examples include:

1. *Mary, the mother of Jesus*: She could've chosen to say "no" when the angel asked her to allow the Holy Spirit to impregnate her outside of marriage; especially because she knew she could be rightfully kicked out of her family or killed because of it. Mary must've sensed a profound destiny in the request. Luke's gospel portrays her feelings in Luke 1:46-55 when Mary erupted into praise after arriving at Elizabeth's home (her cousin) who was also pregnant with John the Baptist.

2. *Abraham*: When the Lord asked Abraham to leave everything he knew behind to head towards an uncertain land, he could have stayed where he was and lived in wealth until he died. He chose to walk forward in faith, and now he is recognized by every Jew and Christian as the standard for faithfulness.

3. *Joshua*: The first mention of Joshua is in Exodus 17:9 when Moses tells him to lead the Israelites into battle with Amalek army. After that, every decision Joshua made was based upon the Lord's vow to deliver the promised land to his people. Also, when Moses asked Joshua to be his assistant, Joshua could've avoided that responsibility and simply maintained the same type of life everyone else had while traveling the desert. His obedience was absolute both to Moses and the Lord, until finally he was named as Moses' successor upon his death.

4. *Esther*: After she became Queen to a Persian King and settled into her role, her Uncle asked her to use her influence to save the Jewish people from a plot to destroy their race. In the Persian culture the King could execute anyone who approached him without

permission, and Esther knew that. She had a choice to make: ignore the plight of her people or consider that the Lord put her in that position "for such a time as this" (Esther 4:14). Because of her radical obedience, not only were the Jews saved, but her Uncle was elevated into a higher position of authority within the Persian Kingdom.

5. *David*: It took almost 15 years from the time he was anointed as King while Saul still reigned to the time he took the throne himself. During most of it, he was on the run for his life, had to live in caves, and experienced many other difficulties. At any point he could've walked away from his destiny, but he didn't which is why David is listed in the faith hall of fame (Hebrews 11:32) and considered a man after G-d's own heart (1 Samuel 13:14).

6. *The Disciples* - Before Jesus approached each of the disciples to follow him, most them had typical family responsibilities and some sort of vocation to make a living. Each one chose Jesus over their cultural expectations based on many generations before. By all appearances, it was crazy to give up everything and follow a man they hardly knew. And yet all of them, except Judas, went to their death praising the Messiah rather than denying who He was to save their lives.

7. *Saul/Paul:* He was an extremely respected Pharisee and Jewish leader who rigidly upheld the law. The first mention of him in the Bible is Acts 7:58 during the stoning of Stephen: "Then they cast him out of the city and stoned him. And the witnesses laid down their garments at the feet of a young man named Saul." After a transformational encounter with Jesus in Acts 9, the Lord commissioned Saul

to bring the Gospel message to the Gentiles. Saul then adopts the Greek name Paul and becomes the largest contributor of authorized scripture in the New Testament. Paul's life was not easy in the least, and he could've walked away in frustration and exhaustion many times. Yet throughout his Epistles he describes over and over how proud he is to have sacrificed the life he could have had for a life sold out to the Lord.

It's hard to imagine walking in the shoes of the people I just mentioned because it's basic human nature to avoid pain and suffering under any circumstance. We also love to cling to as much control of our world as possible. Choosing radical obedience means we must give up all control to the Lord and be willing to suffer - even unjustly - should the Lord allow it to happen. No one willingly does that unless they have a deep level of trust in the person asking them to make that choice.

You cannot develop that level of faith in someone unless you've been through enough "foxhole" circumstances to have it tested and consistently proven true. That's what happened to me over the last 10 years. I had numerous "foxhole" circumstances in my life where I was forced to depend only upon the Lord to get me through them.

Even though a long season of brokenness caused me to lose faith in the Lord for a short while, the "comeback" foxhole circumstance was the turning point to increase my faith to a level I had never experienced before…despite the Lord not fixing my situation. That new level of trust that appeared became a stepping stone towards the radical obedience I needed to say yes to the Lord's invitation to go on this crazy Adventure.

Looking back, I can't imagine what my life would be like today if I had not experienced every moment of that "crazy" journey. My life is enriched because of it and it has laid a solid foundation for whatever the Lord has for me next.

A "normal" life is not even remotely acceptable for me anymore. I've seen too much, and my expectations of the Lord are much higher than ever because I know that freedom in Christ means living my life full-out for the Lord however He asks, and whatever that means - even when it makes no sense to the people who love me most. It's much more important for me to be obedient to the Lord than to receive approve from anyone around me.

You have the same Holy Spirit inside you that Jesus had access to. This passage originally recorded in Isaiah 61 was used by Jesus in Luke 4:18-19 as a proclamation of His position as Messiah; and I believe it can also become a proclamation for us today to fully embrace His Spirit as His Disciples on the Earth: "*The Spirit of the Lord is upon me, because he has anointed me to proclaim good news to the poor. He has sent me to proclaim liberty to the captives and recovering of sight to the blind, to set at liberty those who are oppressed, to proclaim the year of the Lord's favor*" (ESV).

Take a moment and think about what your life could look like if you spent time in prayer seeking the Lord's will for your life in this season, and then committed to being radically obedient to whatever He asks of you.

For some of you, it's no mystery what the Lord wants. You have just been too afraid or selfish to say yes. For others, your heart is in the right place, but you have no clue what that could look like for you and your family.

Here's what I know: the Lord will never invite you into something He isn't willing to prepare you to do through

Him; and if you are married or have a family, He will always provide a way for all of you to walk out His assignment together, individually and as a family. All it requires is a leap of faith, yes and amen!

If you are ready to take a leap of faith and step into radical obedience with the Lord, take a moment and say the prayer below. If you are not yet ready, but want to be, say the 2nd prayer. And if you are not even near wanting to be ready, skip the rest of this chapter and move onto the next chapter.

No judgement! I promise! It's a process to desire that level of radical obedience, never mind choose it! Take a deep breath and just flip to the next chapter. The Lord sees your heart and I promise He has more than enough grace and mercy to wait until you are ready for that depth of relationship with Him.

<u>Radical Obedience Readiness Prayer:</u>

Lord Jesus, I am ready to be radically obedient to your will for my life. I know the plans you have for me are good and you always honor those who honor you. If you have already shown me what you want from me and I missed it, please send me another message and help me to clearly recognize it. If I recognized the message when you sent it, but avoided taking the next step, I repent and will bravely move forward in some way as evidence of my commitment to be radically obedient to you.

Thank you in advance, Lord, for the provision you are setting up to support the path you have asked me to travel. Thank you also for the people you will put in my way to guide me as I move forward.

I am ready to live an extraordinary life through radical obedience and trust any suffering I may experience (through another person's free will or divinely allowed in order to prune my character) will not be wasted. I trust it will serve to make me stronger over time. I love you, Lord, and fully surrender my will to you however that looks.

<u>Desire for Radical Obedience Prayer</u>

Lord, my heart wants to say "yes and amen" to a life of radical obedience, but I don't yet have the courage to do so. I know with you all things are possible. Therefore, I ask for an increase of courage to take the next step towards living a radically obedient life with you. I give you permission to develop that courage in me through whatever circumstances you see fit. Thank you, Lord, for honoring my prayer.

I'd love to hear what happened if you said either of those prayers. If you are comfortable sharing, email your story to me at Kris@BeginToShift.com.

Chapter 16 - Hello & Adventure Update

<u>*September 3*</u>

I had an interesting ride from North Dakota to Washington state due to a challenge with the car. Check out my latest video to hear all about it!

To access Video link, go to:
http://BeginToShift.com/crazy-blessing-videos

Chapter 17 - Car Update & A Gift!

<u>*September 12*</u>

After another unexpected layover, here's my latest video with an update on the car and a gift I received. Enjoy it!

**To access Video link, go to:
http://BeginToShift.com/crazy-blessing-videos**

Chapter 18 - Tethered To Jesus

<u>*September 16*</u>

Hello everyone! I had a fantastic time in Vacaville, CA with my host family, and absolutely loved being a part of The Mission's Wednesday night service. I've been downloading their podcasts for almost a year as spiritual food to develop more intimacy with the Lord. Pastor Gary Hopkins is currently doing a series called "Encounters with the Bridegroom" based on a book he wrote in 2017.

It was wonderful to be there in person and meet Gary and his wife, Karissa, after listening to them teach for a long time. Gary and I had a great conversation before the service started. I shared about my Adventure and told him how much I've enjoyed being a virtual member of their congregation.

The best part of the night was at the end of the service when Gary had everyone stand on each side of the middle aisle so he could walk through and pray over each of us. He asked the Lord to impart a healing anointing for a supernatural ability to set people free from whatever addictive "baggage" (emotional, mental, physical, behavioral, etc.) they carry around which is preventing them from experiencing what the Lord intended for their lives.

When Gary reached me, his prayer included that anointing but expanded it to include all the people the Lord would place in my path during my Adventure. I'm so honored to have been there to receive the anointing in person and can't wait to see how the Lord sets me up to walk that out from this point forward throughout the rest of my life.

As I mentioned in my last video blog, I have been taking photos throughout my journey. As I looked over them recently, one caught my eye and reminded me of a journaling conversation I had with the Lord on 8/27 while I was in Sioux Center, IA.

To give you some background on that part of my trip, I arrived late the night before and spent the next day resting and catching up on emails and blog comments before I had to get ready to give my testimony at the CR group in that town. Earlier that morning there was a heavy rain storm with high winds throughout the area. After it was over, I remember looking out my hotel window and seeing a flag whipping around on the building next to the hotel.

As I watched the flag wildly moving in all directions, this is the conversation I had with Jesus in my journal:

(Kris) "Lord, I am feeling just like that flag outside my hotel window - wildly flapping in the wind with no discernible pattern or stability. As I look at the flag, the only stable part is the side anchored to the pole wire. You are like that pole wire, Lord. You are my constant security, no matter how much the world and my circumstances shake me up or whip me around. "

(Jesus' Reply) "I am your security, Kris, and as long as you keep tethered to me, even your worst circumstances will have a sense of peace because you'll know I am working everything out for good. Don't worry about money or where to lay your head at night. Just keep moving until you are invited to stay, then let me lead you in how to minister to those around you until I prompt you to move on again. I love how you don't do anything half way. You have totally surrendered your heart to me during this Adventure, even though at times you've worried about what's next. I see your heart and I know your intention is to step out boldly with me…and you will as long as you focus on me and not your present situation. You are my warrior woman, Kris. When challenges and impossible situations come at you, lean into me, raise your spiritual sword and boldly say: 'Adversity, come! Give me your best because you will not defeat me. The Lord is my shield and defender, and I have nothing to fear!'"

(Kris) "I will, Lord. You know I love a great Adventure story and I desire to live through you.

Help me to discern accurately where to focus my time and energy, and highlight people around me whom you want me to serve. Thank you for the flag metaphor too!"

****

That journal entry has been a great reminder throughout my travels, especially when there have been financial concerns about how to pay the bills that didn't disappear when I left Atlanta. Each time I started to become worried about those bills, I chose to hand my worry over to the Lord and trust He's going to take care of it. And He always does!

The most recent example was on 9/14. I had three bills to pay totaling over $800, and I had no idea how to make it happen based on the amount of money I knew I had in the bank at that time. But later that day when I checked my bank accounts, I noticed $500 had been deposited into my business account from the consultant I work for part-time. That amount was significantly more than the check I expected. Then when I reviewed my personal checking account, I noticed the gas donation checks I was given a few weeks ago were still in the account (I thought I had already spent that money).

By the time I calculated the money I needed to pay my bills and the money I had available in both accounts, the Lord once again filled the gap! He even gave me an excess of $40 as a cushion in my personal account! HALLELUJAH!

Not only that, but He also timed it so the $450 car mechanic and tire bill from earlier this month would land on the October credit card statement instead of the September one. Whew! I have chosen to peacefully journey forward in my Adventure trusting the Lord will pay that bill too in a divine way. Don't you love how the Lord honors us when we remain obedient in our faith and trust in His provision!

Blessings and favor to all of you! Thanks again for the prayers and check-in emails over the last few weeks!

Until next time! ~Kris

Chapter 19 - Look In Another Direction

September 18

Hi everyone! I spent the afternoon walking around Huntington Dog Beach along the California coast today. It was so much fun watching big and little dogs of all ages enjoy the beach with their owners!

I took this video in a quieter section of the beach (no dogs to show you), but if you want to check out their website to see dogs having fun, here's the link: www.DogBeach.org.

Enjoy my update and the story about the latest lesson I learned.

:) ~Kris

To access Video link, go to:
http://BeginToShift.com/crazy-blessing-videos

Chapter 20 - One HOUR At A Time!

<u>*September 28*</u>

I've been in Dallas, TX for a few days now visiting extended family. Before that I had a scenic drive through Arizona (including magnificent Sedona) and New Mexico, stopping at two fantastic CR groups along the way. Afterwards I spent a few days at a friend's house in Amarillo, TX and gave my testimony at a CR group there.

This morning as I woke up, I was suddenly aware of how weary I feel from the toll of being in the car for most of the past two months. When I left Atlanta, my mileage was 232,188. My mileage as of today is almost 241,000. That's about 9,000 miles and I still have several thousand more miles to go (at least)!

Part of me still loves the excitement of traveling through each state, seeing the countryside for the first time, and the deep fulfillment from stopping at CRs to be a source of encouragement to everyone in the room who is still walking through the torrential storms of their own personal circumstances.

The other part of me eagerly awaits having a stable place to live back in Atlanta until the Lord answers the promise He made to me years ago so I can finally move forward in that part of my life. But most of all, I want what the Lord wants because I know His plans for my future are so much better than my own!

The last two weeks of my Adventure have been interesting. Throughout the journey the Lord has been significantly shortening the time frame of His revelation for where to go next. It seems He no longer wants me to live one day at a time, but rather one HOUR at a time! I say that in jest, but in all seriousness, it's been somewhat uncomfortable for me to have to tell my family or a friend that I need to stay for longer than I expected because the Lord hasn't shown me what direction to move towards next. I know they probably don't care if it's a day or two longer, but part of me feels like my integrity is at stake because I don't want to outstay my welcome or have them feel as though I'm taking advantage of their hospitality.

That very situation happened this week too. When I arrived in Amarillo, TX last weekend I had been trying to line up CRs for my drive from TX to FL with no success…which is why I'm still in Dallas two days past my expected departure date. Similar to my Los Angeles experience, once I realized my desired travel plans were not working out, I recalculated and looked in other directions hoping that was the reason for the delay. I tried contacting different CRs in Louisiana and southern TX, but that didn't work out either. It seemed no matter what direction I tried, all I got was silence.

I decided the Lord was trying to teach me something, so I asked Him for clarification and headed out to dinner to introduce my cousin (4th or 5th removed) named Jimmie Lynn to my aunt (my father's half-sister) named Jimi Sue. They had been hearing about each other for decades through my Dad (their common connection) but had never met because my Dad's side of the family had a split two generations ago which caused several generations of extended family to be unaware of each other. When I found out that Jimi Sue lived only 15-minutes from Jimmie Lynn (whom I was staying with) in the Dallas area, I knew the Lord had given me a divine opportunity to finally close the gap and get them in the same room for the first time over dinner.

Jimi Sue and I arranged to meet before dinner to catch up since it had been about five years since we had seen each other. As I was sharing my Adventure stories, including all the Celebrate Recovery groups I had stopped at to give my testimony, Jimi Sue asked if I had contacted any CRs in Dallas. I said "no" because I wanted to focus on spending time with her and Jimmie Lynn.

It suddenly dawned on me that the Lord was delaying my departure because He wanted me to give my testimony to a Dallas CR group. I pulled out my phone and went to the CR app to see what meetings were available within a 25-mile radius. I showed it to Jimi Sue and asked her if she was familiar with any of those locations. She pointed out a group in Carrollton, TX near her home that was meeting the next day (Thursday). I took a chance and left a voicemail on the church office phone for the CR leader telling her I was available to give my testimony if they wanted me to. Jimi Sue said if it worked out, she'd plan on attending with me to hear my testimony.

Jimmie Lynn arrived at the restaurant a little while later. It was great watching them give each other a hug and see the delight on their faces as they finally met in person. During dinner we traded family stories and shared the "colorful" generational connections we all had in common. I sent a picture of the three of us with the caption "Family Reunion" to my Mom, Dad, and Jimi Sue's step-brother (whom I've known for years), receiving fun replies that they wished they could've been there too. I'm so glad I was finally able to introduce them to each other.

Thursday morning I got up and wondered if the CR opportunity in Dallas was going to come through. I sent an email to the CR leader the night before to follow up, requesting that they let me know by 12 PM and left the decision in G-d's hands. By 1 PM I had not heard anything, so I texted Jimi Sue to let her know so she and I could grab dinner again that night.

At 3 PM I got a call from a number I didn't recognize, hoping it was one of the CRs from south TX or Louisiana. To my surprise it was the CR leader from Carrollton, TX apologizing that her internet had been out for days until just an hour ago. She had gotten my email only a few minutes before and asked if I was still available that night because they had planned a video testimony and would much rather have a live one.

I laughed jovially and agreed to stop by because only the Lord could've coordinated the timing of her internet coming back on just a few hours before their meeting started (especially because the church had not yet relayed my voicemail to them, so the CR leader had no idea I had called the night before). I told her I would be there at 6 PM for their group dinner to get to know everyone before the main event.

Do you see what I mean about one HOUR at a time? :)

The Lord must be training me for something important to keep reducing the time frame in which He communicates with me. I'm guessing He's testing my willingness to trust Him and maintain a good attitude despite not knowing all the information.

It's now Friday morning and the Lord has still not given me any direction for where to go from Dallas. Based on my new "one hour at a time" lesson, I've decided to head towards the gulf coast tomorrow in faith. If no CRs contact me to stop by as I travel in that direction, I'll just grab a hotel for a night and continue East until the Lord opens a CR group or makes it clear about what my assignment is as I head towards FL. I look forward to seeing how it all works out and will blog about that next time.

I'm still feeling somewhat physically tired and yet spiritually energized. This Adventure is truly exciting as I watch to see how the Lord shows up and shows off in all my circumstances.

Here's a verse for those of you who are feeling a bit weary yourselves: "Come to me, all you who are weary and burdened, and I will give you rest. Take my yoke upon you and learn from me, for I am gentle and humble in heart, and you will find rest for your souls. For my yoke is easy and my burden is light" (Matthew 11:28-30).

If there's one thing I'm certain of from this Adventure experience over the last two months, the Lord does provide rest for our souls when we lean into Him instead of focusing on our challenging circumstances. I hope that provides some comfort to you!

Chapter 21 - DRIVE By Faith, Not By Sight!

<u>October 7</u>

I shared at the end of my last blog post that the Lord had not given me any direction for where to go from Dallas. Based on my new 'one hour at a time' lesson, I decided I would leave on faith the next day and head south towards Houston and the Gulf Coast surrendering completely to whatever the Lord would do.

About two hours into my drive the Lord prompted me to call one of the Houston CR leaders I had contacted previously through voicemail and email. I pulled over and called Cindy, but she did not answer. I left another voicemail and kept heading South, completely at peace with receiving a Yes from that CR or continuing towards FL and getting a hotel later that day. My deep level of peace, despite the uncertainty, was a clear indication of how much deeper my faith had grown since leaving Atlanta to go on this "crazy" Adventure on July 22nd.

As I continued down the highway towards Houston, I heard my cell phone go off with a text notification and glanced at my GPS alert. It was Cindy. I listened to her text message, smiled and called her back. When Cindy answered her phone, she said she and her husband had just gotten out of a CR leadership meeting where they had been praying for more live testimonies. She then apologized for not receiving my previous voicemails or my email. She said they would be glad to have me give my testimony to their CR group on Sunday night and arranged for me to stay at one of the other leader's homes both Saturday and Sunday.

I laughed when Cindy said she did not receive my email or phone calls, because I knew the Lord had been testing my obedience and trust in Him over the last 24 hours to see if I would "Drive by Faith, Not By Sight" (a personalized version of 2 Corinthians 5:7). I told Cindy that I suspected the reason she didn't get my messages was because the Lord was doing a heart and attitude *check within me to see how I would respond by withholding that information until I drove south in faith.*

As I changed my GPS to the address of the leader who was hosting me, I thanked the Lord for being a great Daddy, and headed to Houston to get to know more of my amazing CR family.

The time with my host, the CR leaders, and my CR family in Houston over the next two days was a lot of fun. As I prepared to leave, the Lord once again did not provide any information about my next stop despite emailing and calling two CRs in Louisiana. I left in faith, heading east towards FL wondering what would happen next.

After four hours on the road and still no response from the Louisiana CR, I pulled over to get a cup of coffee and started checking the map to gauge where I could get a hotel. I figured I had about four hours of daylight left and decided to make a hotel reservation in Mississippi figuring there must be a reason for the Lord to not open a CR that day.

Just as I started giving my credit card information to the hotel, a call from the Louisiana CR leader came in. I told the hotel I would call them back and switched calls wondering if I had rushed ahead of the Lord by getting a hotel.

Within 30 seconds I knew my spiritual intuition to get a hotel had been accurate because the Louisiana CR Leader informed me they already had a lesson planned for their meeting, appreciated my offer to give my testimony, and wished me well on the rest of my journey. I thanked the Lord for confirming what I had suspected and called the hotel back to finalize the reservation.

After looking at the map again, I noticed the hotel was only about 10 hours from my mother in FL, so I called her next to ask if I could arrive a few days earlier than expected, and she said yes. It was great to settle into the next leg of my trip with clarity about my destination.

After 12 hours of travel the following day due to traffic and stops, I arrived in FL Wednesday evening exhausted but very happy to see my Mom for the first time in two years. Thursday morning I was still tired, but smiling at being able to stay in one place for almost a week - a rare treat for me during this Adventure. As I spent time with Jesus lounging with a cup of coffee in one hand, my journal in another, and fully enjoying the private screened in porch, it suddenly occurred to me that the hotel stay and the early arrival to my mother's house was the Lord's answer to my "weariness" prayer from my last blog post.

The only commitments I had while in FL were driving three hours to visit my brother on Friday, and then returning on Saturday to Mom's home so I could give my testimony at a CR near her place on Sunday. Monday and Tuesday were open days to relax, catch up on work and prepare for my long drive back to Georgia for a training I had to attend, followed by house-sitting for a friend the next week.

I thanked the Lord for His FL gift and smiled even wider. Later that day Mom took me to a restaurant on the beach. It was a lot of fun. I'm very blessed to include Mom in my circle of friends as well as having her as a parent.

Earlier that day when I was lounging outside, I was reflecting on all the things that happened during my G-d Adventure Sabbatical. This "Crazy" road trip is exactly what I needed to prepare me to step into the destiny the Lord has planned for the next season of my life. I know I sound like a broken record, but I really am so glad I said YES to the Lord when He invited me to go with Him!!

So far, I've racked up over 9,000 miles and spoken at more than 18 Celebrate Recovery groups across the country. As you know, the whole trip has been Holy Spirit led with amazing Holy Spirit provision every time I needed a place to stay or money to cover gas, bills, and other expenses. Whenever I needed something, it showed up!! Living "one day at a time" (and sometimes one hour at a time) has been the best decision I ever made!

Every day Matthew 6:25-34 has become more and more real to me. Especially this section: "Therefore do not worry about tomorrow, for tomorrow will worry about itself. Each day has enough trouble of its own." My daily choice to surrender my tomorrows to the Lord - regardless of how difficult my circumstances - and focusing only on today has truly given me an abundance of peace.

I still have no idea if my stop in GA next week is the end of my Adventure or whether I'll just be passing through to continue on with it. I suspect the Lord will make it clear to me before the end of October. I look forward to seeing how that works out too!

Chapter 22 - 11,000 Miles In 3 Months!

<u>*October 18*</u>

Hi All! For those of you wondering why there has been such a long delay between my last blog post and this one, I apologize. I had to stay a few extra days in FL due to Hurricane Michael causing road closures on I-75. Because of the delay I've been playing non-stop catch up ever since I arrived back in GA, followed by a week of onboard training for a coaching company that has contracted me as part of their national team of coaches. They are hoping to ramp up enough new business for all of us to receive clients by early next year.

I'm still adjusting to being back in Georgia after being gone for so long. Since I left on my Adventure, I've driven almost 11K miles in just about three months with stops in 18 of the 26 states I drove through! WOW!!

Is the Adventure over now that I'm back where I started? I'm not sure. The Lord has not yet provided me with a steady stream of income to sign a lease or given me any clarity of what's next. A friend has graciously given me a room to stay through October 31st so for right now I'm still focusing on my theme song, "One Day At A Time." If it doesn't involve today, I continue to practice surrendering everything else by saying "that's tomorrow's problem" and trusting the Lord to take care of it.

I still get frustrated at times because I'm wired to find answers and solve challenges. Learning to surrender and rest in the Lord has been an interesting journey. But thanks to Celebrate Recovery and my Adventure over the last three months, I am now capable of shifting into "rest" mode more quickly.

Remember my first blog where I hosted a contest for the best guess of the total mileage I would reach when I returned to GA, offering a prize of a coaching meeting for whoever came closest? My mileage at the beginning of the Adventure was 232,188. Several people gave a wide range of predictions, but the nearest guesses were Laure Hoffman who said 241,000 and Ike Ikokwu who said

248,888. When I returned my odometer read 243,027. Since Laure came closest, she'll be receiving that gift before the end of the year (CONGRATS, LAURE!!).

I'll send another blog post in early November to let you know if I'm officially back in Georgia or if the Lord wants me to keep going.

I have been sensing the Lord leading me to speak at churches and other faith-based organizations or conferences using my Adventure story as a platform to showcase the Lord's faithfulness and share all the lessons I learned along the way. My "crazy" experience is sure to give hope and encouragement to people in difficult circumstances, deepen their faith, and provide an opportunity for them to experience the Lord in a new and transformational way.

I'll keep you posted as to how all that works out. Thanks for keeping me in prayer as I rest in the Lord and eagerly await His direction. :)

Chapter 23 - The Adventure Continues

<u>November 2</u>

After arriving back in GA with a steady place to live for three weeks, I was elated to finally unpack my car and actually have my own space for an extended period of time without having to constantly move my stuff from place to place. I also found myself wresting with the Lord about having to continue the Adventure if He asked me to.

As I began to catch up with friends in the Atlanta area, they all asked me if I was back for good. There was a definite weariness in my voice when I responded each time with the words, "I don't know" followed by a sense of being homeless, and a vague attitude of entitlement in wanting the Lord to open a door for me to stay in the area.

I realized I was struggling with a Matthew 6:1 challenge: "For where your treasure is, there your heart will be also." I had a choice to make. Would my treasure be the comfort and convenience I long for in having a place of my own in Atlanta, or is my treasure solely the Lord and what He desires to do with my life for His glory and Kingdom impact wherever He leads me?

I knew what the right answer was, of course, but surrendering what I wanted in exchange for what the Lord wanted from me was an internal process over a few days. It's not that I didn't want to submit to the Lord's leading, it was simply that I was tired of traveling so much over the last few months.

After journaling my feelings with the Lord, He responded by saying, "Beloved child, wrap your arms around me and all will be well no matter where you are. You are not homeless, but moving about in my house. Surrender your wants and hopes to me, and I will take care of them until they can be birthed into reality. For today, do what has to get done and just enjoy visiting with your friends. Remember, tomorrow is my concern."

I smiled and realized the Lord had quoted part of the prophetic word I received from a lady at the

Middletown, NY Celebrate Recovery group back in July (see the blog post titled "Joy"): "You are not homeless, not homeless. For heaven is the Lord's and the earth His footstool. So, in the days ahead as you go from one place to the next, know that you are not homeless. You are just moving about and around in His house."

How could I argue with that? The Lord clearly wanted the Adventure to continue so I went down to my storage unit, swapped out summer clothes for winter clothes, got rid of anything I wouldn't need, and prepared to rest and see a few people before I headed out on the Adventure again.

I called a friend I hadn't seen in years who lived in the Georgia mountains. She said I could stay with her for two days. I decided to use the same routine of contacting CRs within 250 miles of my location to see which doors the Lord would open for me from there. I'm guessing I'll be on the road for the rest of the year since I need to be in FL around Christmas to help my Mom move. But, of course, that's up to the Lord. My job is to focus on only ONE day at a time! :)

The only thing I do know is the Lord wants to use the testimony of His provision and guidance during my Adventure to help people deepen their faith, have more Kingdom impact within their sphere of influence, and provide hope and encouragement to those in difficult circumstances. So, if you know of any faith-based groups who could benefit from that message, let me know. Thanks so much! :)

The last thing I want to share is that I received my 18-month Celebrate Recovery chip when I stopped by my home CR group this week. It's amazing to think that eighteen months ago I was broken emotionally, spiritually and mentally due to an extremely painful circumstance I had been going through for years, and truly wondering at that time if I would ever experience the joy and peace the Lord promises to all of us in scripture.

Choosing to get involved in Celebrate Recovery and their 12-step program was the first shift toward receiving those promises. Now, 18-months later, I still can't believe how joyful and at peace I am on a regular basis despite the instability of my life at this time. Thank you to Celebrate Recovery and the wonderful women who walked with me through that journey as the Holy Spirit guided me towards healing and wholeness!

I head back on my Adventure on 11/8/Thu. As I travel onward, I'll keep updating my blog with new G-d stories as they occur and continue adding my destinations to the G-d Adventure Map to show you where I've been.

I'm nearing 11,000 miles so far. I wonder what the final total will be whenever the Adventure is really done? :)

Have a great rest of your day! Blessings to each of you!

**To View the G-d Adventure Map, go to:
http://BeginToShift.com/crazy-blessing-videos**

Chapter 24 - Manna From Heaven

<u>November 11</u>

As a testament to my obedience in continuing the Adventure with a good attitude, the Lord showed up and showed off before I left Georgia the second time. I also have a provision story from before I returned to Georgia that I still need to share. I continue to be astonished at how creative the Lord can be in how He chooses to deliver "manna from heaven" to ensure I have what I need when I need it (for those of you unfamiliar with the manna story, read Exodus 16 where the Lord provided bread in the form of manna to the Israelites during their 40-year journey).

Before I tell those stories, I need to go back and share the abundance of manna I received between Arizona and Texas. While traveling through those states I spoke at several CRs and visited a few friends and family. At various times the Lord prompted several people to give me cash gifts to pay for gas, food, and any other needs I had. I kept those cash gifts in an envelope, and one day I noticed it had gotten really thick.

As I counted the money, there was almost $600 which was an unusual amount to accumulate. For most of the Adventure the Lord only gave me enough of a cushion financially to travel between a few places. I didn't know what the Lord was planning or what He saw ahead of me, so I placed $50 in my wallet leaving the rest alone until the Lord revealed its purpose.

In the "DRIVE By Faith, Not By Sight" blog, I shared that I arrived at my Mom's house a few days early and went out to dinner with her at the restaurant by the beach. What I didn't mention in that blog is on the way to the restaurant as we passed a Chase bank on the road, I felt a strong sense in my spirit that the Chase bank was important. However, I didn't know why because I don't have a Chase bank account. Later I totally forgot about the bank and went to bed.

The next morning the internet was out in the neighborhood, so I had to go to a coffee shop with internet *access to get some stuff done online. As I pulled up to Panera Bread to hang out for the day, a Chase Bank was in the same complex. Again, I felt the Holy Spirit prompt me to go to the bank. I parked the car in front and asked the Lord why the bank was important. Then the answer suddenly became clear.*

In September when my car broke down in Washington state, I didn't have money to pay for it. I charged both the mechanic bill and the four new tires (totaling $450) on my credit card trusting the Lord would figure out how to cover the cost when the bill came due during October. That credit card was a CHASE credit card, and the bill was due in two weeks.

I instinctively knew the Lord had supplied the abundance of cash between AZ and TX to cover that bill. I went into the bank to make a $450 cash payment on the credit card, silently thanked the Lord for covering the cost, and then praised Him all day for honoring my obedience through that provision.

Today as I am writing this blog post I am laughing because I just realized this moment the Lord set up the Panera Bread next to the bank as a loving metaphor of His "manna" in my life.

Now for my second story, which is even more amazing:

After being back in Georgia for two weeks in mid-October, I realized the Lord had not released me from the Adventure. Even though I was very disappointed, I obediently went to storage to swap out summer clothes for winter ones because the weather was getting cooler in Georgia and I didn't know where He would send me next. I also wanted to unload the stuff in my car that I didn't need.

While at my storage unit I took out a large envelope I had used to store a variety of cards I received from people throughout my travels thanking me for my CR testimony or wishing me well on my Adventure. I started taping those cards into my journal as keepsakes, and then I noticed the first card I was given back in July from my CR step-sisters and other friends from my home CR location.

I strange thing about it was that the card was bulky. I remember it being flat when I stored it in my backpack just before I left on my Adventure. As I opened the card, a wad of bills fell out: $273 - the exact amount they gave me when I received the card BEFORE I left on my Adventure as a departing gift. SERIOUSLY!!!

I looked at the cash in awe because I know I put that money in my purse three months ago when I left Georgia to pay for gas and food on my way to NY, and would've blown through that amount quickly with all the traveling I had done over the next few weeks.

The only explanation I could come up with is a supernatural one: the Lord divinely replaced the exact amount I received from my CR family before I left Georgia as His confirmation that I was making the right decision to continue the Adventure; and that He would continue to provide what I need, when I needed it each mile of my journey. I love that He did that for me even though I struggled with surrendering to His decision before I knew what it was.

If you've been following my blog posts over the last few months, I hope the stories I've shared have given you more confidence in your ability to trust the Lord with the needs in your life. He loves you as much as He loves me, and will certainly provide for you as well if you surrender your life to Him and trust Him with everything you have.

I challenge you today to surrender something you've been stressing about for a long time. Take a few minutes to lay it at the Lord's feet. Then choose to walk away trusting He WILL take care of it, giving Him the freedom to meet that need the way He desires, rather than attaching any expectations to His provision.

If you start stressing and feel the need to take it back, surrender it once again to the Lord; even if you must do that 100 times the first day or the first week. When you remain committed to leaving it at His feet, at some point you'll find yourself trusting more and struggling less, until one day you'll realize you really do trust Him with that situation and have a deep peace that He'll take care of it.

If you take me up on that challenge, I'd love to hear your surrender stories and how the Lord took care of it despite your shaky trust in the beginning. When you see evidence of the Lord working things out for you, send an email (Kris@BeginToShift.com) to me. I look forward to reading it.

Here's a great verse to remember as you take a leap of faith to begin the challenge:

"May everyone who knows your mercy keep putting their trust in you, for they can count on you for help no matter what. O Lord, you will never, no never, neglect those who come to you" (Psalm 9:10).

Blessings and favor to all of you! ~Kris :)

Chapter 25 - Family & Friends

<u>*November 20*</u>

It's been about a week and a half since I left on the second part of my Adventure, and I've had fun visiting more family and friends.

I arrived in Blue Ridge, GA on 11/8/Thu. I haven't seen Steve and Kathy for a few years. They were part of the church I belonged to in Snellville, GA from 2004-2012. I was thrilled the timing worked out to visit them, especially because I wanted to see the fruition of a promise the Lord made to Kathy a long time ago.

Like most promises from the Lord, it's important to hold onto them as absolutely true, but loosely cling to the timing and the exact interpretation because sometimes we don't have all the information at the time we receive the promise. For example, when Kathy received her promise from the Lord, she thought it was about opening a bed and breakfast (B&B) business. But as they continued towards retirement over the years the B&B business didn't fall into place, so Steve and Kathy continued to pray for the Lord to receive further revelation.

It wasn't until they bought their retirement home over 15-years later in Blue Ridge and started building that they realized the Lord wanted their home to become a B&B environment (not a business) for people in difficult situations to have a safe place to heal, rest and recover. To fulfill that purpose, they built guest bedrooms on the bottom floor of their mountain home with access to their lower deck, and now their home is a wonderful ministry for each guest that arrives.

I stayed with Steve and Kathy for two nights and three days. We had so much fun catching up, and the food was amazing (Steve made Bananas Foster for dessert…YUMMY!!). One afternoon Kathy took me to the village shopping area and we had time to walk around and see all the neat shops before it poured.

The one thing I didn't expect during my visit was the drastic drop in temperature to freezing the day I left. It was quite a surprise to go out to my car and find all the locks frozen, along with hearing the trunk lock click open but not be able to get in because of the frozen water around the seals from the rain the day before. I had to wait an hour for the temperature to rise enough to open the trunk before I left. Memories of NY winters came to mind, and I'm truly glad I don't have to deal with freezing temperatures that often in the south!

Before I left Blue Ridge, Steve and Kathy had me sign their guest book and take a picture next to their outside sign to add to their collection of visitors over the last year. The word "Gotteshaus" on the sign means "God's House"…and theirs certainly is! I look forward to coming back another time to visit!

After Blue Ridge, I headed over to Chattanooga, TN to see extended family. Remember Jimi Sue from the "One HOUR At A Time" blog post? Steve is Jimi Sue's brother. I met Steve, his wife Cindy and their daughter, Allison, about 10-years ago. They've always been fun to hang out with.

We spent a majority of the weekend trading stories about our lives. Because it was rainy and very cold for most of my visit, the following week Steve took me on a scenic tour of Chattanooga in his car over Signal Mountain and drove around the hairpin turns on W Road. The drive was absolutely beautiful, and I can't wait to come back in the Summer with my motorcycle to do it again ((though I may avoid W road. I would be nervous riding it in my car, let alone my bike!).

While I was in Chattanooga, I also had an opportunity to give my testimony at a Celebrate Recovery group in Soddy-Daisy, TN. As always, the Lord divinely arranged for someone to be there to hear my story as a boost of encouragement and hope in their circumstances. It was a great night and a wonderful time meeting more of my CR family!

My next stop was Huntsville, AL to see a lady I used to work with when I lived in Florida. She moved to Alabama to be near her family two years ago and I told her that at some point I would head over from Atlanta to say hello. Of course, this Adventure allowed that to happen sooner than I expected. I enjoyed spending time with her and meeting her family, as well as hearing the latest updates of all the people we used to work with in FL.

After that I headed to Guntersville, AL to stay with a lady I got to know on LinkedIn, but never actually met. We've stayed in touch via phone, FB and email for over a year. I had never been to that part of Alabama before. It was a beautiful lake community and I truly enjoyed driving around the area.

After experiencing miserable cold and rain for two days, it finally warmed up enough for me to go to the walking trail around the lake. I spent about 45-minutes enjoying the scenery and listening to Praise and Worship music. There were lots of ducks walking around or swimming in the lake. They didn't even scatter when I walked near them, so I'm guessing they are used to having people around and probably enjoy meals from them as well!

A few days later I headed to Hayden, AL to see a lady I've been wanting to meet for three years! Without even knowing it, Brenda significantly impacted my walk with the Lord and I've been so thankful for that transformational moment in my life ever since. Here's that story:

Back in 2015 I attended a Proverbs 31 Ministries Online Bible Study. During one of the Facebook Live events, they were talking about praise and worship music being an important part of a Believer's life. I publicly commented that I didn't connect to how others enjoyed praise and worship music and tended to show up late during a church service to miss it so I could focus on the sermon, which was my favorite part.

Brenda happened to see my comment and private messaged me on Facebook to share her experience of why praise and worship music had been so significant in her life. We traded emails to continue the conversation, and then she suggested I get a book called "Exploring

Worship - a Practical Guide to Praise & Worship" by Bob Sorge. I felt the Lord prompt me to get the book, and I'm so glad I did. It provided both the educational side and Spiritual benefits I needed in order to understand and FINALLY GET IT!

After I finished the book, I began to spend time on a regular basis worshiping the Lord by myself (thank the Lord for Pandora!!) which began a season of deepening my connection to the Holy Spirit, followed by the development of many spiritual gifts I had always heard about, but had never flowed in at that time.

Today I absolutely love praise and worship music and rarely go a day without spending time with the Lord either by myself or in a community setting. I can't even imagine my life without praise and worship time!! Thanks again, Brenda, for following the Lord's prompting to reply to my comment three years ago. And also for your willingness to share your life story to help me understand the importance of praise and worship.

A fitting close for this blog post is Psalm 138, a psalm of praise by King David (Complete Jewish Bible version):

I give you thanks with all my heart. Not to idols, but to you I sing praise.

I bow down toward your holy temple and give thanks to your name for your grace and truth; for you have made your word [even] greater than the whole of your reputation.

When I called, you answered me, you made me bold and strong.

All the kings of the earth will thank you, Adonai, when they hear the words you have spoken.

They will sing about Adonai's ways, "Great is the glory of Adonai!"

For though Adonai is high, he cares for the lowly; while the proud he perceives from afar.

*You keep me alive when surrounded by danger;
you put out your hand when my enemies rage; with
your right hand you save me.*

*Adonai will fulfill his purpose for me. Your grace,
Adonai, continues forever. Don't abandon the work
of your hands!*

Happy Thanksgiving, everyone! :)

Chapter 26 - The End Of Me

<u>November 17</u>

I am currently back in Georgia, quite unexpectedly, sitting in the room I used to rent thanks to the graciousness of my previous landlord, Kimberlee, who offered to let me stay for two weeks until her new tenant moved in.

My arrival back in GA had quite a bit of confusion attached to it. When I left on my Adventure for the second time I assumed it would be the same routine: Contact CRs along the route I was taking based on the night they met, give my testimony at their group, stay at someone's home afterwards, move onto the next CR, and repeat throughout the Southeastern states until mid-December when I planned to head back to FL to help my Mom move into her new apartment.

That was my expectation. However, it did not turn out that way. Regardless of the emails and phone calls I made, and despite numerous attempts to adjust days and locations to find CRs as I traveled around GA, TN and AL, the Lord opened only one CR while I was visiting with my family in Chattanooga, TN.

Since nothing I was doing seemed to be working the way it did during the previous journey, I realized the Lord was keeping me in a holding pattern for a reason only He understood. Before I left GA the second time, Kimberlee mentioned her home was available through November if I needed it, and because of the extended struggle to land CR groups, I figured I should take Kimberlee up on her offer until I figured out what the Lord wanted me to do next.

After unpacking my car and settling in at Kimberlee's home the Monday before Thanksgiving, I spent a lot of time being introspective and wondering why the Lord was allowing so much ambiguity despite not releasing me from the Adventure when I returned the first time in mid-October.

It was strange. I was very clear on the purpose the Lord had for the first part of my Adventure. But when I left the second time and that same purpose didn't play out, I spent most of my traveling between GA, TN and AL in a fog of confusion wondering what the Lord was up to.

On Tuesday morning I spent time journaling with the Lord about my confusion and desire for clarity. I felt the Lord telling me that I didn't need to know the purpose for this part of my Adventure. He just wanted me to wait for Him to open doors and trust that the seeds I plant by carrying His presence wherever I am will have Kingdom impact, even if I never know what those seeds produce. When I got that answer from the Lord, I'll admit I was disappointed. It was a lot easier to maintain excitement about my Adventure when there was a tangible purpose guiding me.

During that same journaling conversation, the Lord also told me that part of the reason for His silence about my purpose is because He wants me to arrive at the end of myself. At first I didn't really get what He meant because I was obediently following His leading by continuing the Adventure and doing the best I could to look for opportunities to help others around me. I was also maintaining my "one day / one hour at a time" mindset trusting in His provision. What else was left for me to arrive at the end of myself? And what did the end of myself look like anyway?

I thought about that the rest of the day, and the next morning I spent time journaling with the Lord again. He provided a bit more insight, though not the full picture I was hoping for.

Here's an overview of our conversation:

<u>Kris</u>:

Lord, I have been meditating on "coming to the end of myself" and sense it's about surrendering even more deeply to you, along with a willingness to die to myself in all areas of my life. Lord, what information do you want to share about that to lead me forward in the path you have placed before me?

118

<u>*Jesus:*</u>

Daughter, think about the TV series that you've been watching lately about a medieval kingdom. It has been full of examples of people sacrificing their personal desires for the greater good of something else or because of loyalty to another. Just like those characters, you are my Warrior - loyal, faithful and true to my will in your life and those around you. You honor me as your King, and you fight for what's right based on the promises I have given you. I know your heart and am so proud of you, my child.

There are still a number of battles ahead of you to see those promises come true, and some of those battles will bring uncertainty and cause you pain - but you will endure and you will see those promises come to fruition.

Like any Warrior in a battle, you must be completely focused on your King's strategy and plans. If you don't know what they are, you must seek me for direction and follow those directions even if they don't make any sense in the natural world because I see the larger picture - you see only a small piece.

If you waiver between your desires and my directions, you will slow down your progress. So you must come to the end of yourself to be fully in tune with me. Be willing to give up all your desires for a stable place to live and financial security. Get to a place of being content with living one moment at a time, trusting in me.

You are so close, Daughter! I know you are at a place of peace right now. What I would like is for you to get to a place of contentment without a time frame of release; that will be a sign of you arriving at the end of yourself. Saying "Yes" and "Amen" to every door I open or close is part of that.

Choose to die to yourself in all things, Kris, because dying to you gives me more freedom to work through you in a powerful way. Keep meditating on my words and all will become clearer day by day. I love you, Daughter!

****

I spent the day pondering what Lord said to me, and the next day I had another journaling conversation with Him:

<u>*Kris:*</u>

Lord, I desire to reach the next level of surrender, and yet I know the "tests" to get there will certainly cause a number of conflicting emotions within me, which is part of my pruning process. Help me to quickly recognize those growth moments so I can proceed through them easily. What additional information do you want to give me about "coming to the end of myself"?

<u>*Jesus:*</u>

Precious Daughter - dying to yourself is not about being a doormat. Have no fear of others taking advantage of you continuously. It's about what I want to do in a situation (not what the other person wants), and how you can demonstrate my love, grace, and mercy to them when they need it most.

You are a vessel for my power, words, and deeds to flow through. Your effectiveness is only as good as your ability to let me flow through you without the obstacles of self-will. The less your will gets in my way, the more impact I will have in that moment.

You have done a great job of creating healthy boundaries with others. What I am asking is for you to be willing to lay them down for the greater good of a person or situation as a sacrifice for me…but only when you know I am asking that of you. Otherwise keep those healthy boundaries in place. My peace inside you will help you make those decisions and my grace will suffice when you get it wrong. I know your heart, so don't worry about making the wrong choice. I will always work it out for good.

****

A day later during the next journaling conversation, I gained even more clarity about why the Lord had altered this part of my Adventure to include so much down time:

<u>*Kris:*</u>

Lord, what do you want me to do next? I still feel aimless in this part of my Adventure. What do you want me to focus on?

<u>*Jesus:*</u>

I want you to focus on me, Kris. I have plans for you which will require deeper intimacy with me than you've experienced previously. Use the time at Kimberlee's and the extended time with your Mom in December to write your book about this Adventure and all the things you learned along the way. Other than that, just focus on being with me through worship, prayer, and journaling. Your time over the rest of the year is not wasted, even though you may feel like that. Nor are you being delayed from the destiny I have for you in the next season of your life. You are exactly where you should be.

You are still striving to figure out your future. I promise, Kris, it will be revealed when it's time. If you have what you need today, then rest fully in me. You are naturally driven to achieve, but this is not the time for achievement. REST, Kris. All will become known and doors will open in my time.

<u>*Kris:*</u>

Okay, Lord. I willingly choose to surrender my future again and will continue to do so whenever the desire to strive for answers eats at me. I trust you and your perfect timing, even though my human nature wants to make it happen now. Love you, Lord!

****

I took the Lord at His word, laid down all desires and expectations of my future, and began writing my book. Thanksgiving was in a few days. Since I had arrived back into the area unexpectedly, I did not have any plans for the holiday (Kimberlee was out of town celebrating with her family). After all the traveling I had done over the last few months, I was perfectly content having the house to myself, relaxing, and binge-watching shows I had not seen in a while.

However, I did mention to the Lord that it would be great if I had a Thanksgiving dinner invitation to consider should I feel like getting out of the house. And just like a good Daddy, He delivered one the next day from Kimberlee's best friend, Nicole, whom I knew as well. If the Lord was going to deliver an invitation that quickly, I figured He wanted me there, and I'm glad I went. I had a wonderful time getting to know Nicole's family and friends over a delicious meal and great conversation.

As I finish up this blog post I am continuing to work on my book and preparing to leave on Friday for Florida to see two friends, followed by a visit with Mom until the end of the year so I can help her get settled into her new apartment. I assume by then the Lord will open a door for me to step into the next season of my life or make it clear where He wants me to travel next. Based on my conversations with the Lord, I am choosing to focus only on today and leave all my tomorrows in the Lord's capable hands.

A fitting closing for this blog is John 1:9-18 (CJB) which proclaims the birth of Messiah:

"The true light, which gives light to everyone, was coming into the world. He was in the world, and the world was made through him, yet the world did not know him. He came to his own, and his own people did not receive him. But to all who did receive him, who believed in his name, he gave the right to become children of God, who were born, not of blood nor of the will of the flesh nor of the will of man, but of God.

And the Word became flesh and dwelt among us, and we have seen his glory, glory as of the only Son from the Father, full of grace and truth. (John bore witness about him, and cried out, "This was he of whom I said, 'He who comes after me ranks before me, because he was before me'"). For from his fullness we have all received, grace upon grace. For the law was given through Moses; grace and truth came through Jesus Christ. No one has ever seen God; the only God, who is at the Father's side, he has made him known."

I'll blog again when there are more updates as more G-d stories occur. Until then, I wish you all a very blessed holiday season!

~Kris

Chapter 27 - Last Post ??

<u>December 10</u>

Hello everyone! I arrived back in FL on 11/30/Fri. My first stop for the weekend was a friend named D'Anna. What's really funny is several times during 2017 and 2018 when she lived in GA, we tried multiple times to get together for coffee at her home and it never worked out with either of our schedules. I had to wait another year and drive over 400 miles to her new home in FL to make that happen. :)

We laughed about that several times while I was there. The wait was well worth it too! Great conversations, hilarious moments with her kids, and a fun discussion with her and her husband. I look forward to doing it again at some point in the future.

Sunday morning I left to drive another 400+ miles to meet a friend named Rindi who used to be in a women's small group I attended in GA from 2012 - 2014. When I found out she now lived 90-minutes North of my Mom it proved to be a great opportunity to reconnect.

Over dinner we shared all the things that had happened in our lives since 2014, discovering several similar experiences. I'm so glad she reached out on Facebook to let me know where she was living a few months ago. I arrived at my Mom's place later that evening and was thrilled to be able to settle in and write my book over the next couple of weeks.

The FL destination during this part of my Adventure seems to be another gift from the Lord. It's 70 degrees most days, which is my favorite type of weather. Before I left GA, the temperatures ranged between 20 and 50 degrees, so you can imagine how happy I am to be down here enjoying the sunshine and heat rather than the cold.

As of today, I'm almost done writing my book. I'm excited about getting it published early next year so I can share the testimony of the Lord's faithfulness throughout my Adventure and all the things I learned along the way.

Thanks to all of you for the words of encouragement and the prayers you've offered at various times throughout my journey. I've loved having you follow me through my Adventure and I hope you've benefited in some way from the stories I've shared.

This may be my last post unless the Lord prompts me to send another one. If not, Merry Christmas and Happy New Year to all of you! May Blessings and Favor follow you around for the rest of your life!

:) ~Kris

Chapter 28 - My Interview :)

<u>December 13</u>

Hey all! It turns out I have another post to share.

I was interviewed today by Carol Dunlop for her business podcast about how my "Crazy" adventure has impacted my life and my business. It turned out well, so I wanted to share it with all of you.

Feel free to pass on the interview link to anyone you think could benefit from it.

Enjoy! ~Kris

**To access Interview link, go to:
http://BeginToShift.com/crazy-blessing-videos**

Chapter 29 - Who Do You Think You Are?

Do you ever wonder why the same problems seem to follow certain people throughout their entire lives? In my younger years I didn't understand why that happened until I heard someone say, "He (She) can move across town, change jobs, or divorce and remarry another. It won't matter. You take yourself with you wherever you go."

Mahatma Gandhi echoes that concept in his statement, "Your beliefs become your thoughts. Your thoughts become your words. Your words become your actions. Your actions become your habits. Your habits become your values. Your values become your destiny."

Joyce Meyer wrote a book called *Battlefield of the Mind*[5] which also alludes to that very theme. She says, "So many people are rooted in thinking patterns that actually produce the problems they experience in their lives….The mind is a battlefield. It is a vital necessity that we line up our thoughts with God's thoughts" (p 12).

Within that battlefield lies an identity question: *Who do you think you are?* Your words, decisions and actions will generally correspond with who you believe you are today or who you are trying to become tomorrow. If they do not correspond, chances are you have a blind spot which needs to be acknowledged and shifted as the Lord leads.

For instance, if you believe you are fearless, your actions will reflect that by the risks you take and the decisions you make. On the other hand, if you believe you are fearless, but second guess everything you do, your true identity is probably closer to fearful rather than fearless.

---

[5] Meyer, Joyce. <u>Battlefield of the Mind – Winning the Battle in Your Mind</u>. New York, NY: Warner Books, 1995.

A perfect example of an identity problem can be found in the book of Exodus. Even though the Israelites witnessed Moses part the Red Sea and they watched the Lord drown all the Egyptians who came after them, they continued to act and speak as though they were still slaves. After the golden calf incident (Exodus 32), the Lord knew they would not be capable of capturing the land He promised them until their identity was grounded in Him, which is why they ended up spending 40-years in the desert developing that identity.

Throughout my lifetime I've learned my identity will either carry me through or crush me when difficult circumstances arise. That is why I maintain a circle of godly men and women who have permission to speak truth to me, even if it hurts to hear it.

What identity are you currently carrying around as you move toward the land the Lord has promised you? Is your identity serving you well or do you need to adjust it? If you cannot confidently answer that question, find a godly friend or family member who can help you process through it.

Your true identity should always be grounded in Christ and all the promises He made for you on the cross. No matter what is happening in your life right now or what mistakes you've made in the past, this is who you are in Christ:
- Beloved (Jeremiah 31:3)
- Free (Galatians 5:1)
- Whole (Colossians 2:10)
- Never Alone (Deuteronomy 31:8)
- Victorious (Psalm 18:35)
- Bold (2 Corinthians 3:12)
- Wonderfully Made (Psalm 139:14)
- Delighted In (Zephaniah 3:17)
- Made New (2 Corinthians 5:17)

- Forgiven (Luke 6:37)

I could keep going, but I'm hoping you get the point!

You are amazing, and don't let anyone tell you differently - no matter what has happened in your past. *You are a Son or Daughter of the Most High G-d, so act like it.* If you have any doubts, a great book to help reinforce your identity in the Lord is a devotional by Neil T. Anderson called "Who I Am In Christ."[6]

Always remember you are a NEW person in Christ. Paul reminds us of that in Colossians 3:9-10: *"Never lie to one another; because you have stripped away the old self, with its ways, and have put on the new self, which is continually being renewed in fuller and fuller knowledge, closer and closer to the image of its Creator."*

Take a minute and ask the Lord to give you a personal encounter this week to show you how true that passage is.

---

[6] Anderson, Neil T, Who I Am In Christ. Ventura, CA: Regal Books, 2001.

Chapter 30 - Be A Box Breaker

Everyone has invisible boxes they carry around inside of them which directly affect how they act and react. Some of those boxes relate to your identity (as mentioned in the last chapter), and other boxes focus on the people or organizations you interact with regularly.

For example, inside me I have many invisible boxes with the names of people I know well: family, friends, co-workers, groups I belong to, etc. Each box contains my perceptions of all the previous interactions I've had with those people which prompt me to respond to them in a familiar way each time.

Those boxes work really well for me…until the day they do not. I remember once I was catching up with a long-time friend and she was telling me about several decisions she had made over the last few years. As she began to share her reasoning behind those decisions, my brain struggled to process her words and my invisible box for her began to shatter.

Her decisions had no impact on my life. Yet because I had no frame of reference for her actions within the box of perceptions I had carried around throughout our entire relationship, that box soon became a damaging obstacle between us. If that invisible box had not existed, I would have done a much better job being a loving friend rather than a critical judge during that conversation (thankfully, I eventually recognized it and apologized).

The flip side has also been true for me. I had a box in my head containing all the times a particular person had failed me. Each time I tried to give that person the benefit of the doubt, they would fail me again and reinforce the contents of the box I carried around inside my head. Then one day that person went out of his way to come through for me, which totally caught me off guard. A few weeks later it happened again, and then once more a few months later.

My invisible box no longer held the truth. As that box cracked and fell apart, I struggled with how to move forward in our relationship because my box provided a safety buffer between us as justification to keep this person emotionally at arm's length. Interacting with this person who didn't fail me consistently was a foreign concept that took a long time to get used to.

Another one I discovered this year was a G-d box. I had no idea it even existed until the Lord invited me to pack up my stuff and go on an Adventure with Him. It didn't matter that I had grown by leaps and bounds in my spiritual walk over the past two years. It also didn't matter that I knew the Lord worked in mysterious ways as indicated in Proverbs 3:5-6, "*Trust in Adonai with all your heart; do not rely on your own understanding. In all your ways acknowledge him; then he will level your paths*" (CJB).

The invisible G-d box inside me rebelled completely against that invitation because it seemed crazy. It also caused me to stubbornly refuse to adjust my perceptions until the Lord graciously gave me several signs to lovingly point me in the right direction of His will for my life.

I have come to realize I must honestly acknowledge all the invisible boxes I carry inside me and work really hard to keep them flexible. Doing so gives me the ability to love others well as the Lord directs from circumstance to circumstance rather than rigidly treating someone the same way all the time. It also allows the Lord to open opportunities for me to experience the abundant life He desires to give me.

Another lesson I've learned is to destroy my G-d box all together because His thoughts are not our thoughts and His ways are not our ways (Isaiah 55:8-9). As we develop intimacy in our walk with the Lord, we should not automatically discount the "crazy" things we sense or see in our spirit. Instead, we must look at them with spiritual eyes and ask the Lord for confirmation to proceed in that direction.

The Lord always wants the best for us and will lovingly prune anything which interferes with that (John 15:1-11). Take a minute to review the last few years of your life. Are there invisible boxes you currently carry around which may not be serving you well? The last time your box reared its ugly head, did you allow the Lord to break that box or did you reinforce it with extra lining and place a triple padlock through it that still exists today?

Don't feel judged. I am aware of at least one or two boxes inside me that I haven't fully relinquished to the Lord. It's not essential for me to do so right now, but I sense it will be within the next year to avoid creating unnecessary obstacles during the assignments the Lord is preparing for me next. I am ready to work through the process of laying those boxes down when the Lord says its time to do so. That's progress! :)

How about you? Are you brave enough to ask the Lord to help you break your boxes to see what He has on the other side of them? If so, say the following prayer and watch how the Lord honors your willingness to surrender another part of your life to Him:

Lord Jesus, you knew me long before I was in my mother's womb, and you know every bit of my story from beginning to end. That divine and perfect perspective makes you the best person to determine what I need and who I need to be in every season of my life to receive all the gifts you have for me.

Help me to relinquish every box inside of me that is not serving me well. Give me the courage to lay them down and allow you to do the inner work necessary to reframe those perspectives and remove those limitations so I can step out more powerfully in my life and work.

Thank you, Lord, for loving me so much that you refuse to let me stay as I am. I willingly give you permission to do whatever you have to do to transform me into the person you want me to be.

Amen.

Chapter 31 - Kingdom Impact

In chapter 15, I mentioned, "The Lord is in the business of Kingdom Impact to bring as many people into the family of Believers as possible before Jesus returns to the Earth to bring us all home (Revelation 19). Kingdom Impact is more than just sharing the Gospel with others. The deeper our intimacy with the Lord, the more likely He is to shine brightly through us no matter what we are doing on any given day. Our very lives become a testimony to Him without having to say a word."

Before we were even conceived, the Lord had a plan and purpose for our lives: *"For we are of God's making, created in union with the Messiah Yeshua for a life of good actions already prepared by God for us to do"* Ephesians 2:10 / CJB). The people He places around us and the circumstances we journey through all become layers of Kingdom Impact opportunity for His glory.

Within our sphere of influence lies very fertile ground for us to partner with the Lord in completing the assignments He's prepared for us to do. Sometimes we even get to see the seeds of that impact grow into something beautiful. Other times we don't even realize how our words or actions affected the life of another person (even a simple smile at a stranger may make all the difference in his or her world).

As we mature in the Lord, we start to notice more often how He strategically puts opportunities in our path to benefit the people around us. It may be offering to babysit a single mother's children as a gift to give her a well-needed break. It could be buying a meal for the homeless person you pass on the way to work every day, or taking someone out for lunch to show them how much you value them.

Sometimes the assignments are more complex like the teenager in the neighborhood who always seems to be getting in trouble because he doesn't have a father in his life to guide him into manhood. Or possibly the negative neighbor who complains about everything because she's never had anyone love her well.

Then there are the assignments which on the surface feel unbearable, but you know that you know the Lord has called you to stand firm in Him during that assignment as He transforms that circumstance in a way only He can do.

Your sphere of influence runs deep and wide throughout your personal and professional life. The impact you can have for the Lord's Kingdom is enormous if you keep your eyes and ears tuned to the Lord as you move about your day. All that's required is your willingness to be used by Him.

Earlier this year I had been praying for the Lord to expand my impact in His Kingdom and was diligently listening for His voice to guide me to those opportunities. One of my favorite stories is the day I drove to my storage unit. As I punched in my code to open the gate at the storage facility, I noticed a man and woman sorting through their stuff in one of the units nearby. Their younger children were running around playing and their older daughter was standing next to their truck.

I didn't think anything of it until I felt a deep wave of compassion go through me as I passed by them in my car. In my spirit I could sense the family was going through a really hard time. Then I felt the Lord tell me to stop and let the family know that He sees them, and He loves them very much. My compassion quickly turned to discomfort because they were complete strangers and I had no idea how they would receive that message. I hesitated for a split second and then continued driving to the back of the facility to my own unit.

As I parked the car, the Lord reminded me of my "Kingdom Impact" prayer and lovingly told me I was responding to that opportunity from a place of fear rather than the boldness He knew I had inside me. He asked me again to go back and give that family His message. I wavered between obedience and discomfort for another minute, realizing this was a defining moment in my spiritual growth. I grabbed what I needed from my unit and drove back to the front of the facility hoping the family was still there.

As I pulled around the corner and saw them still sorting through their stuff, I exhaled in relief. Still uncomfortable, I parked the car behind the family's truck, walked over to their unit, took a deep breath and said, "This may sound strange, and I don't know what your situation is, but as I drove past you earlier the Lord asked me to stop and let you know He sees you and He loves you very much." I held my breath as I waited for their response.

The father's eyes softened, and the mother's eyes began to tear up. Their response changed my life forever.

"We just lost our home and I also lost my job. Three weeks ago, we accepted Jesus as our Savior. We have no idea where we are going to live, and I've been trying to have faith He will provide for us," said the father.

The mother, wiping the tears from her eyes, followed with, "Thank you so much for telling us that. You don't know how much it means to us."

Then their little boy turns to me and says, "Did Jesus really tell you to say that to us?"

I laughed and turned to him with a smile saying, "Yes He did. He loves you and your family so much He arranged to have me be here at the same time as you so I could give you the message."

I silently asked the Lord what else He wanted to tell this precious family, and these words popped into my head, "The Lord wants you to know He's working things out for your family. I don't know how long it will take, or how it will look, but trust He sees you and knows your needs. He will provide for them in His perfect way and His perfect timing." Then I asked if I could pray for the family and they said yes.

We got into a circle, held hands, and I asked the Lord for an abundance of blessings to be showered on their family and that He would continue to show them His presence daily as they waited on His provision. At the end of my prayer I asked if they had money for dinner. The father looked at the ground and quietly said, "not much." I knew I had $20 in my wallet, so I handed it over and apologized for not having more. Each member of the family gave me a hug and thanked me for stopping by.

As I drove away, I repented to the Lord for almost missing an opportunity to bless that family. I also recognized the Lord purposely arranged for them to be brand new Believers was to show me the importance of diligently following His instructions instead of doubting them. My decision to be obedient helped build that family's faith, and in turn it also built mine. A win-win Kingdom Impact moment!

The story of the five talents comes to mind as I reflect on that experience (Matthew 25:14-30 and Luke 19:12-28). The lesson Jesus provided through that parable is that we must take responsibility to steward what He has already given us (or told us) before He will give us anything else. In other words, *to whom much is given, much is required."* (Luke 12:48).

Have you stewarded the opportunities the Lord has previously given you within your sphere of influence?

Actions speak much louder than words. In my own story, the words of my "Kingdom Impact" prayer did not actually prove anything other than good intentions until I was willing to follow through with the actions required to be obedient in response to that prayer.

Don't forget, you have numerous opportunities to expand your Impact for the Lord within your sphere of influence. Merely look around at the people you see and consider all the situations you are connected to. Write down the people you connect with regularly (your immediate and extended family, neighbors, hobby groups, work, community groups) and each situation they are going through (especially the challenging ones in your neighborhood, communities, local organizations, etc.). Then prayerfully ask the Lord the following question:

"Lord, what role do you want me to play in this person's life or in this situation? Show me what you want me to say or do and give me the courage to diligently follow your instructions."

If you don't have a journal, buy one to record the opportunities the Lord places before you over the next few weeks. Write down a brief description of the situation, what you said or did as led by the Lord, and how it turned out. Not only will that journal give you a running testimony of your faithfulness to the Lord in each situation, it will also provide a tangible reminder of the Lord's ability to provide for you whenever your life becomes challenging.

For those of you who are truly serious about having more Kingdom Impact, here is an additional prayer you can offer to the Lord: *"Lord, who in my life can lovingly hold me accountable to my Kingdom Impact prayer so I don't shy away from following through with what I know you want me to do?"*

I leave you with a promise from Galatians 6:9 (ESV), *"And let us not grow weary of doing good, for in due season we will reap, if we do not give up"* and 2 Timothy 1:7 (ESV), *""For God gave us a spirit not of fear but of power and love and self-control."*

As your journal begins to fill with Kingdom Impact stories, feel free to share them with me if you are comfortable doing so (Kris@BeginToShift.com). I'd love to hear them!

Chapter 32 - Serenity

The only prayer that seems to come close to the popularity of The Lord's Prayer is a prayer written by Reinhold Niebuhr in 1943. Bill W., the founder of Alcoholics Anonymous (A.A), included a section of Niebuhr's prayer in his book, "A.A. Comes of Age." The power and wisdom of that prayer (renamed as "The Serenity Prayer") quickly became a part of the A.A. culture, and it has remained so ever since.

The Serenity Prayer became an important part of my life almost two years ago. At the end of each Celebrate Recovery (CR) meeting, we would read that prayer together as a group. The leaders also encouraged everyone to read it on a daily basis to support the recovery progress we were striving towards within our individual circumstances.

At various points in my recovery journey, different sentences and words of that prayer became a focal point to step into my next stage of healing. As I share the words that significantly impacted me (bolded below) and what was going on in my head at that time, ask the Lord to show you the areas of your life that He desires to heal:

<u>THE SERENITY PRAYER</u>

*God, grant me the **Serenity** to **accept** the things I cannot change.*

> After years of living in a rollercoaster of brokenness, serenity felt unattainable, yet desperately desired. The first few weeks I attended CR I begged the Lord to give me serenity. Then one day I realized serenity came only when I accepted the things I

could not change. Serenity would not come by asking to receive it.

*The courage to change the things I can, and the **wisdom** to know the difference.*

I had to learn how to get out of my own way and wisely discern the line between what was my responsibility to change within my circumstances, and what I had to let go of. I'm a natural troubleshooter, which is a great quality when striving towards a goal, but can become quite a hinderance when the actions of another are far outside my control.

*Living **one day** at a time, enjoying **one moment** at a time;*

At the beginning of my recovery journey I was angry, exhausted, and shattered spiritually. All I wanted at that time was to fast-track past the pain and arrive at the healing stage as quickly as possible. Focusing on only one day or one moment at a time was a rough process of surrender. It took many months before daily surrender became a lifestyle. Once I reached that point, I discovered incredible inner strength to successfully maneuver through all kinds of uncertainty, which eventually laid the foundation for my "crazy" Adventure with the Lord.

Accepting hardship *as a pathway to peace.*

I hated this section of the prayer and used to cry each time as I said those words. The reason why I ended up in CR was because of the crushing hardship I had endured for years. I felt it was cruel for the Lord to require that I accept my hardship,

141

and I couldn't imagine how doing so would become a pathway to peace. Over time as my healing deepened, I began to understand that staying resentful or angry at my hardship did nothing to make it better. Peace began showing up only after I accepted my hardship as it was (since I couldn't change the past which led to it), along with leaning into the Lord to show me how to overcome it.

*Taking, as Jesus did, this sinful world **as it is**; Not as I would have it;*

I didn't like my world as it was - not one bit! I also didn't like the person who was the cause of my suffering. It took a while, but as I began to understand that free will is a gift from the Lord to everyone, it became easier to accept other's free will "as it is" despite the hurtful ways they may wield it. I had to believe the Lord would deal with that person as He saw fit, and that my responsibility in each hurtful situation was to rely His strength to act lovingly as I dealt with a variety of their sinful responses.

*Trusting that You will make **all things right** if I **surrender** to Your will;*

Before CR, I experienced a season where I lost faith in the Lord and questioned his character many times. I wanted to believe He would make all things right and surrender to His will. However, all I felt was bitterness and resentment towards the Lord. The 12-step program and the weekly CR meetings provided a systematic way for me to process through my emotions, re-build my faith and reframe my perspective of who the Lord is in any situation, trusting He will work everything out for good, eventually.

*So that I may be **reasonably happy** in this life and supremely happy with You forever **in the next**.*

As my trust in the Lord was restored and my surrender deepened, all my emotional anguish shifted to joy over time. I had found inner peace through leaning into the Lord, accepting my circumstances as they were, and wading deeply into His Holy Spirit healing power. My circumstances did not change, but I certainly did from the inside out! THAT is what made all the difference as I continue to wait for the Lord to honor His promise to me with regards to my situation.

****

I hope what I shared above is helpful to you. Find a copy of the Serenity prayer online. Read it at least once a day and listen for the lessons the Lord wants you to learn as you move with Him into this next season of your life.

Chapter 33 - Ready For Your A.D.V.E.N.T.U.R.E ?

As I put the final touches on this book, my situation remains the same: The Lord has not yet released me from my Adventure and I am still moving from place to place as the Lord prompts people to open their homes to me for a day, a week, or longer. Financially, I don't have a clue how the bills will be paid, but I remain at peace and deeply rooted in the One who does know, believing the money will show up when I need it.

I miss having a home with all my stuff around me and a cushion of money in the bank. And yet this Adventure has completely transformed my perspective of what a "normal" life looks like from the Lord's perspective.

Thanks to everything I have learned on my "Crazy" Adventure with the Lord, my new "normal" is whatever He says it is while living my life one day at a time - however that looks. In this season, "normal" is living out of my car while trusting in His complete provision. Next season it will be something else. As long as my security is in the Lord rather than what I have access to or what I am capable of doing, I'll always be fine.

Don't get me wrong, my desire is for the Lord to release me from the Adventure into a stable residence with abundant financial resources. Whenever feelings of frustration or sadness overwhelm me, I hand them to the Lord and we process through them together. My willingness to be honest with Him is one of the reasons I can maintain the inner peace and joy I receive from the Holy Spirit on a daily basis.

Like any relationship grounded in trust, hard conversations are necessary to grow into deeper intimacy with others. The Lord is no different. Being "real" gives me the freedom to come to Him as I am (in any state of mind), and it provides the opportunity for me to listen to whatever is on the Lord's heart, even if it's difficult to hear. That type of relationship is rock solid and will survive even in the most difficult of seasons.

You've spent your precious time reading all about my Adventure as you've progressed through this book, Are you ready to go on an Adventure of your own with the Lord?

Each part of my Adventure was specifically designed for me by the Lord in preparation for the next season of my life. My Adventure just happened to require that I physically move from place to place. Your Adventure will look completely different as He focuses on shifting the external circumstances or internal qualities which need to be adjusted for you to step into your next season of life.

External Adventures might look like: a) resigning from your current job and seeking one better suited to your skills and interests, b) moving to a different city to uncover opportunities you will love, but don't even know about yet; or c) letting go of that man or woman you've been seeing and focusing on the Lord for a while to prepare you for the spouse He desires for your life.

Internal Adventures could be: a) attitudes He wants to change, b) emotional healing He desires to complete, c) trust He wants to build, or d) character traits He wishes to develop.

Regardless of what type of Adventure He invites you on, make sure to buy a journal to record your experiences and all the promises or directions the Lord will give you along the way. Similar to the Israelites putting 12 stones in the Jordan River (Joshua 4) as a memorial of how the Lord rescued, directed and cared for them, your journal will also become a living testimony of what He says and does for you.

As I was praying about how to close out this book, the Lord suggested I create an acronym to outline nine potential areas you can focus on as you prepare to take your own Adventure with Him.

You may not feel comfortable with each one, and that's okay. All the Lord asks is for you to have a desire to improve in each area and He will set up plenty of opportunities to strengthen your ability to work it out with Him.

These areas are in no particular order, so prayerfully read through them to discern which one the Lord wants you to start working on.

A.D.V.E.N.T.U.R.E. Preparation

A = All of You (Surrender!!)

> Surrendering "all of me" to the Lord was a process of peeling away layer after layer of self-will until I arrived at a place of profound confidence that the Lord's will was far better than my own. My surrender journey was not easy or quick. Yet once I learned to "let go and let G-d," the choice to surrender all of me became the life-blood of endurance as I walked through a multitude of interesting circumstances.
>
> On this side of my Adventure I recognize how the Lord divinely used each moment of my journey to gently guide me into a deeper level of surrender to Him. I still have many years of life left and I'm sure

there will be many other opportunities to give up more of myself to Him for His glory.

D = Desire for Kingdom Impact

From the moment we are born our desires guide our words, actions and responses. As we grow in maturity, we recognize the danger of letting unhealthy desires grow roots within us and the benefits of focusing on honorable desires which often lead to deep joy over time.

A desire for Kingdom Impact and a commitment to aligning everything we do towards that desire provides the perfect environment to watch amazing things happen all around us. Once the Lord sees that desire deepen in your heart, He will give you many occasions to make a difference for His glory.

V = Voice Of G-d

The Lord is always speaking to His kids; we just need to learn how to tune into the unique frequency He set up for each of us to hear Him. During most of my Adventure I felt like I was walking on a transparent glass floor wondering if I was heading in the right direction and hoping my next step would land on something solid. Because of all the ambiguity, it was essential for me to hear the Lord's voice to stay on the correct path He was laying out each day and to ensure I made decisions aligned with His purpose for the journey.

Do you recognize the Lord's voice in your life? If not, I highly recommend purchasing the book mentioned in Chapter 14 titled "4 Keys to Hearing God's Voice." Another book I read several years earlier which was also helpful in understanding how the Lord speaks to us is "Experiencing God: Knowing and Doing the Will of God (Revised and Expanded)"[7] by Henry Blackaby.

Your Adventure will likely include moments of confusion and important decision crossroads. The clearer you can hear the Lord's voice, the less likely you are to end up on rabbit trails which could cause delays in where ever the Lord is leading you.

E = Empathy

As you grow in intimacy with the Lord, He may ask you to make decisions that align perfectly with what He is doing in and around your life, but seem absolutely "crazy" by the world's standards. Your ability to empathize with others' opinions without having to agree with them is a core quality in effective communication.

I had several conversations like that with many people I knew well before I left on my "Crazy" Adventure. If I felt they were open-minded enough to consider a new perspective, I would do my best to help them understand why I knew the Lord had invited me on an Abraham-like journey. Other times I simply said, "Let's just agree to disagree" because it was clear they weren't willing to consider any point of view but their own.

Another reason to learn how to empathize better is because at some point the Lord is going to ask you to love someone in the midst of the messy

---

[7] Blackaby, Henry. Experiencing God: Knowing and Doing the Will of God (Revised and Expanded). Nashville, TN: B&H Publishing Group, 2008.

circumstances of their life. Jesus was a master at showing others how much he valued them apart from what they said or did in His presence. His loving treatment of them often proved significant in helping them find their way back to G-d and often led to restoring other important relationships.

N = New Territory

Throughout your walk with the Lord, He will open new assignments and blessings as you deepen your relationship with Him and obediently follow His leading. You must not become complacent or too attached to those blessings or assignments because they may only be for a season to lay the foundation for even greater blessings and assignments.

There is an art to finding a balance between tending to your current territory and preparing to step into the new territory you will eventually receive. Keeping your ear tuned to the Lord for His guidance as you manage both is a great approach to achieving that balance.

T = Trust Previous Confirmations From The Lord

When you say "yes" to the Adventure the Lord presents to you, you'll journey through many circumstances to remove your "old self" as the Lord begins to develop your "new self" in His likeness (Ephesians 4:20-24 / ESV). At various points on your journey He will also give you directives and promises to propel you forward. Once you test that information to confirm it is from the Lord (1 Thessalonians 5:19-21), it's important you hold onto it as truth no matter what happens around you.

The devil would like nothing more than to derail your Adventure or cause a major delay in its completion. One of his most effective weapons to interfere with the Lord's plans for your life is to sow confusion and doubt at various points along your journey in an attempt to shatter your foundation in the Lord.

A great parable from Matthew 7:24-27 explains that concept: "*So, everyone who hears these words of mine and acts on them will be like a sensible man who built his house on bedrock. The rain fell, the rivers flooded, the winds blew and beat against that house, but it didn't collapse, because its foundation was on rock. But everyone who hears these words of mine and does not act on them will be like a stupid man who built his house on sand. The rain fell, the rivers flooded, the wind blew and beat against that house, and it collapsed - and its collapse was horrendous!*"

During challenging parts of your Adventure, you will inevitably question if you really heard the Lord correctly and wonder if you are still on the right path. When that happens, pull out your journal. Read through all the promises He gave you and review all the directions He provided previously to alleviate your anxiety and build back your confidence to continue your journey as you lean into the Lord.

U = Unstoppable Despite Inevitable Obstacles

In Philippians 3:12-14, Paul uses a race analogy to describe our faith journey with the Lord. Your Adventure will inevitably have obstacles. When they appear, remember what Paul said in Hebrews 12:1-3 (NIV): "*Therefore, since we are surrounded by such a great cloud of witnesses, let us throw off everything that hinders and the sin that so easily entangles. And let us run with perseverance the race marked out for us, fixing our eyes on Jesus, the pioneer and perfecter of faith. For the joy set before him he endured the cross, scorning its shame, and sat down at the right hand of the throne of God. Consider him who endured such opposition from sinners, so that you will not grow weary and lose heart."*

You are Unstoppable when you lean into the Lord. He will never invite you someplace where He hasn't already ordained your success. It may take several trials and errors (which are often part of your growth process), but eventually you will experience the win He intended all along.

Run with perseverance the race marked out for you, and watch the Lord pave your road with victory after victory as you obediently step forward trusting in Him.

R = Revelation For What You Need

In addition to the assurance of victory, the Lord will also provide revelation about what you need to do or say to maneuver through each circumstance you experience. The more difficult the circumstance, the more important it is to sit with the Lord to receive that revelation.

Throughout the Old and New Testament, you'll find many references to people inquiring of the Lord for guidance in their situations. Why should it be any different today? Running ahead of the Lord can often backfire and cause more problems than the Lord intended during your Adventure.

Establish a daily time with the Lord to receive His revelation. Our knowledge is very limited whereas the Lord's knowledge is limitless. He knows what's coming down our path long before we do, and only He can alert us of divine shortcuts or detours we need as an advantage over our circumstances.

E = Expect The Lord Will Show Up and Show Off

The Psalms are filled with descriptions of the Lord stepping into a circumstance and radically transforming it in a way only He can do. Psalm 77:11-14 is an example of what this looks like: "*I will remember the deeds of the Lord; yes, I will remember your wonders of old. I will ponder all your work, and meditate on your mighty deeds. Your way, O God, is holy. What god is great like our God? You are the God who works wonders; you have made known your might among the peoples.*"

The Lord loves to show up and show off in your circumstances. My blog posts during my own Adventure are a testimony of that. The really neat part was the more freedom I gave the Lord to work out the details of my circumstances however He saw best, the more amazing those situations turned out.

Live in a constant state of expectation that the Lord is always at work around you, no matter how dire your circumstances seem. If the Lord said He would do something, believe He will. If the Lord was not clear about the outcome in a specific situation, honor Him with praise and stand in faith that He will bring good out of whatever happens next even if it crushes you in that moment.

****

In addition to your nine A.D.V.E.N.T.U.R.E areas, I also want to point out that your attitude will be a defining factor in how you experience your Adventure journey with the Lord. You can choose to maintain a positive attitude, having faith in the Lord regardless of the challenges you face, or you can carry around a negative one. It's your choice.

My suggestion is to approach your Adventure with the wonder of a child (Matthew 18:3). No matter what journey the Lord calls you into, arrive full of excitement, curiosity, persistence, imagination, resilience and a belief that anything can happen because the Lord is walking with you each step of the way. Wake up every day with child-like faith in the Lord and watch your Adventure unfold in remarkable ways.

<u>Are you ready to ask the Lord to reveal the Adventure He has designed for this season of your life</u>?

There is no reason to fear the answer because the Lord loves you far deeper and wider than any parent ever could. He knows what you can handle, even if you don't yet recognize it. Within the next day or two get alone with the Lord and say the following prayer with an open heart and hands lifted high in surrender:

Lord Jesus, your Word says you lead the humble in what is right and teach the humble your way (Psalm 25:5). Today I humbly come before you, asking for you to reveal the Adventure you have uniquely created for me as a stepping stone toward the destiny you have ordained for my life.

*I willingly surrender **A**ll of me because of my deep **D**esire to partner with you for Kingdom Impact. I want to develop more clarity in hearing your **V**oice. Transform my heart to have an increase in **E**mpathy towards others, especially if they do not agree with my decision to follow you into this Adventure. Show me the **N**ew territory you are preparing me to receive and help me to **T**rust in what I know to be true based on the confirmations I've previously received from you.*

*With you on my side, I know I am **U**nstoppable regardless of the obstacles that show up at any point in my journey. Help me to prioritize my day to ensure I am spending time with you to receive the **R**evelation I need. Whenever I feel doubt or uncertainty creep in, remind me to **E**xpect you to show up and show off in a way only you can do. Let my attitude be aligned with yours in every circumstance and may child-like faith flow out of me every day.*

I love you, Lord, and look forward to learning what the Adventure is and how to begin stepping into it. Thank you in advance for confirming the details of my Adventure through the godly men and women you have put around me. Prepare their hearts to receive those confirmations and give them the courage to share it with me in your perfect timing.

Your word also says you are faithful and will strengthen me and protect me from the evil one (2 Thessalonians 3:3). I stand on that truth because I know the moment I accept your invitation to embark on my Adventure, the devil will do his best to interfere with the plans you have for my future. Regardless of whether he attacks me or my family, I will not fear or be dismayed for you are my God and you will uphold me with your righteous right hand (Isaiah 41:10).

Thank you, Lord, for the opportunity to take this leap of faith, and bless my obedience as you see fit. AMEN!

Are you as excited as I am for you? I hope so! I look forward to hearing all about it as you feel led to share your Adventure with me.

May the Lord make grace abound to you so that having sufficiency in all things, at all times, you may prosper in every good work (2 Corinthians 9:8)!

Blessings and favor to you! :) - Kris

Adventure Testimonies

"Kris Cavanaugh Castro stopped by Life Church in late October 2018. She was traveling through our area and asked if she could give her testimony at our Celebrate Recovery. At first I was a bit leery, but after reading her story and getting a chance to meet her, I knew God had led her to our group. Her testimony was exactly what several of our attendees needed to hear that night. She spoke with great clarity and you could feel the passion in her words. Her life-story is a true testimony of God's faithfulness. If you are in need of a speaker for an event, or a testimony at your local recovery meeting, I would highly recommend Kris."
– Cindy M., Life Church (Houston, TX)

"I had the pleasure of meeting and housing Kris Cavanaugh Castro for a day over the Summer of 2018 when she spoke at our Celebrate Recovery meeting. Kris was very comfortable talking to our group, interacted well with everyone, and was a positive encouragement to those who spoke with her after the meeting. I have confidence she will do well in whatever she feels God is leading her to do."
– Dana P., Female CR at Leader at Lebanon Evangelical Free Church (Jonestown, PA)

"Kris gave a professional presentation at a Recovery group I work with. She was punctual, positive, and encouraging. She connected well with many of our attendees."
- Seth T., Trained Recovery Coach (Amarillo, TX)

Work With Kris During Your Adventure

As you embark on your Adventure, are you interested in having Kris coach and mentor you through each stage of it?

Kris also loves to work with groups (either on site or virtually through video conferencing) to facilitate an environment for everyone to support and encourage each other during their individual Adventures with the Lord.

Prayerfully consider meeting with Kris to chat in more detail about how to make that happen by calling 404-551-3601 or emailing her at Kris@BeginToShift.com.

Check out Kris' client testimonies at the end of this book.

Why Invite Kris To Speak To Your Group?

Kris Castro is passionate about making a difference in the lives of those around her through giving them hope, encouraging them in their challenging circumstances, and helping them transform their relationship with the Lord in a deeper way. She describes herself as a Faithful Warrior, an Inspiring Visionary, and a Bold Change-Agent after 50 years of walking with the Lord through both joyful and extremely difficult seasons of her life.

Kris's company, Shift Inc.™, creates possibility-rich environments filled with laughter, encouragement, and affirmation leading others to endless growth opportunities. Her programs help others: Realize their identity in Messiah; Achieve the destiny the Lord desires for their lives; Enhance their potential; Increase their confidence levels; and Overcome obstacles more easily to attain their heart's desire in every life area.

Kris absolutely loves coaching, training and mentoring others in a deeply transformative way using the Holy Spirit as her guide.

<u>During Her Presentation Attendees Will:</u>
- Learn the biblical concept of trusting the Lord and surrendering to His will in a deeper way

- Shift from merely experiencing life challenges towards having "adventure opportunities" with the Lord

- Understand the benefits of fully stepping into a Matthew 6:25 lifestyle

- Discover tangible faith growth opportunities both personally and professionally

- (For Sessions Over A Few Days): Experience a deeper dive into all Kris' adventure lessons, and have focused time to determine what their own Adventure with the Lord might be in this season of life

<u>This Presentation Is Great For:</u>
- Ministry Conferences
- Women's Groups, Retreats and Conferences
- Church Retreats
- Christian Professional Groups / Organizations
- Faith Organizations of any size

<u>How To Book Kris For Your Next Event:</u>

Call Kris at 404-551-3601 or email the answers to the questions below to Kris@BeginToShift.com (after receiving your email, Kris will call you within 24 - 48 hours to discuss your event in more detail).

1. How many people will be attending this presentation?

2. Where will the presentation be held? (Event Location Name & City/State)

3. Is this a 60-min presentation or Several Sessions Over A Few Days?

For organizations that do not have a budget for speakers, ask Kris about her "love" offering opportunity :)

Testimonies from groups who have invited Kris to speak previously are included in the next section.

Speaker Testimonies

"One of our IT Managers referred Kris to us as a speaker for our Women of AT&T luncheon. Her interactive presentation proved to be very insightful and valuable to everyone in the room. Several employees thanked me afterwards for inviting Kris to speak and suggested we have her come back for another event. I would highly recommend Kris to any company seeking to motivate their employees to be their best because she has a natural way of helping them "connect the dots" and providing strategic tools to make it happen."

\- Theresa Spralling, Senior Associate Director of Training, AT&T

"On behalf of the U. S. Small Business Administration, I would like to thank you for agreeing to participate as one of the instructors for the "WNET Roundtable." The vast majority of attendees gave the workshop an "Excellent" rating which is the highest rating possible. You presented the topic, "SHIFT-ing from Stuck in Neutral to C.E.O. of Your Life" in a very profound manner. The information imparted to the participants was well received. They are more knowledgeable about cultivating a CEO mindset in every area of their businesses, careers, and personal lives. You played a major role in making the workshop a successful event."

\- Charlotte Johnson, Business Development Specialist, U.S. Small Business Association of Georgia.

"Kris provided an insightful and helpful coaching workshop for my team members. Her ability to immediately connect to everyone made the presentation very easy to follow and interact. She elicited feedback and dialogue which made the time go almost too fast! My team members have all given me feedback that she gave them new tips on

managing stress and time. It was said that they would immediately implement the tools provided during Kris's talk with us. Many have asked to have Kris speak to their direct reports. I would recommend Kris Cavanaugh to any group looking to grow and improve immediately. She will help anyone achieve the business and personal goals they have set for themselves."

- Dr. Pam Hale, Former Regional Manager, Banfield Pet Hospital (a <u>Pet Smart</u> Partner)

"Kris recently spoke at our monthly luncheon, educating our members about how to SHIFT their lives from the norm of feeling powerless, imprisoned, or disillusioned by the many complexities and stresses of life, into becoming the CEO of our own lives and destinies. Her delivery was excellent, engaging, and insightful. I would highly recommend that the next occasion you have to allow Kris to speak to your association or group. Definitely do so, being prepared to look inwardly during and after. Kris poses hard questions that caused us all to examine where we have been, where we are, and where we WANT to go. She rounds that out with HOW to get there… Excellent!"

- Scott Brown, President, Atlanta Chapter of the National Funding Association

"Kris recently conducted a program as part of an Executive Skills Boot Camp for the Kettering Executive Network (KEN). KEN is an executive group dedicated to "Pay it Forward" and Personal Development. During the program Kris shared her SHIFT philosophy and grabbed the attention of all of the 40 participants. Each one walked away with a better understanding of how to develop their own plan to become the CEO of their life. Many of the participants have since commented that Kris' approach is an easy to talk about, but hard to do topic. The "Taking Control of Your Life"

presentation has helped them make tremendous progress. If you are looking for a speaker that is not only inspirational but also give practical, actionable advice, I would highly recommend that you talk to Kris. She did a great job for us and was fun and easy to work with."

~ Michael Robertson, <u>Kettering Executive Network</u>
Program Manager

"We invited Kris to participate in our Annual Staff Meeting to present on the topic of Stress and Time Management. Leading up to the presentation and during the planning process she communicated well. Her delivery was excellent, and she communicated well with our team. After Kris' presentation many of our team members came to me affirming the value they found in the training. She was well prepared for her presentation, yet exhibited flexibility to meet the needs of the audience. Her presentation was interactive. She asked great questions, listened well, and provided insightful practices for dealing with stress and improving time management."

- Jack Bruce, C.O.O., <u>BIS Benefits</u>

About Shift Inc.™

Kris' company, Shift Inc.™, provides coaching and training services to individuals, leadership executives, and teams.

Coaching and Training are often used interchangeably, but they are different styles of development. In a nutshell, training is more about transferring knowledge while coaching is about enhancing knowledge.

Training is driven by the trainer who generally controls the process and is satisfied with providing knowledge and building skills. Coaching, on the other hand, is a facilitated conversation where the coach and client partner to create an environment and a flexible structure to achieve desired professional or personal results.

Coaching does this through helping a person focus their energies effectively; encourages the full utilization of strengths; identifies weaknesses and transforms them into strengths; applies feedback and review of key challenges; and reinforces the behaviors that serve you well to continue progress toward your short and long-term goals.

Both training and coaching do an effective job developing people. However, coaching tends to have longer term results. The ICF (International Coaching Federation) defines coaching as partnering with clients in a thought provoking and creative process which inspires them to maximize their personal and professional potential.

Most clients invest in a coaching program because the journey to achieve their goal or overcome their challenge is often complex and they know they'll fast-track their progress with the support of a certified Coach.

Coaching programs are structured so the Client steers the journey, and the Coach acts as a trusted advisor along the way. It's similar to fictional stories where the main character feels compelled to do something and begins his journey with that goal in mind, but has absolutely no idea of how to make it happen. Because of that, the main character typically asks the person he trusts the most to accompany him on the journey as a second set of eyes, an objective observer, and a companion to brainstorm with.

During Shift Coaching programs, I become that trusted advisor, but I am never in charge of the journey. <u>YOU are</u>. You take the lead and I guide you towards the knowledge and resources you need during your journey, using standard ICF coaching competencies and consulting, training or mentoring as needed.

The best fictional analogy I can think of for a coach/client relationship is Frodo Baggins and Samwise Gamgee from *The Lord of the Rings*. Frodo felt compelled to destroy the One Ring in the fires of Mount Doom in Mordor, but had no idea how to go about it because it was a mammoth task with no clear plan of action. Frodo knew he couldn't do it alone, so he asked Sam to join him.

Sam didn't tell Frodo how to begin his journey or what steps he needed to take. He simply waited for Frodo to make up his mind and followed him onward. During the journey Sam helped Frodo determine the results he wanted, provided insight, asked him questions when he was curious or felt something wasn't quite right, assisted in creating action plans, encouraged him, and held him accountable for his goal, no matter how agitated Frodo got with him along the way.

Sam also helped Frodo see alternatives he hadn't considered, and his mere presence became Frodo's strength when Frodo became too weary and wanted to give up. Overall Sam was the rock (and catalyst) that Frodo needed to achieve his goal. Without Sam, Frodo may never have reached Mount Doom.

One of my main responsibilities as your Coach is to hold you accountable to your goals and "hold your hand" through the change process when forward movement becomes very difficult. I always tell my clients before they start their coaching program: *"The change process will often be difficult and may bring periods of intense joy or intense discomfort. As you are experiencing the forward movement of change, celebrate whichever period you are in because it means you are getting much closer to where you desire to be in your personal or professional life."*

Through my programs:

- I will ensure your success by committing to providing a safe environment in which you can be yourself, and experiment, fantasize, and strategize about your choices without limitation.

- I will challenge you to step outside your comfort zones to tap into your potential.

- I will speak the truth as I see it, even if you do not like what you hear because my job is to ensure that you stay on track with the vision you set at the beginning of our program.

- I will also keep our conversations confidential so that you are free to express yourself however you are feeling in the moment.

- My most successful clients never give up. They push through their fears and difficult circumstances to find alternatives to get what they want no matter how hard their journey.

If you are ready to invest in yourself or your team through a Coaching Program, contact me at 404-551-3601 or go to this link to set up a complimentary coffee and conversation:

www.BeginToShift.com/Make-The-Shift

Client Testimonies

> *"Before starting Kris' program everything looked like it was going well, but internally I felt stuck. Somehow, I couldn't take the steps needed to realize the business dream (which required a change in business model) I have had for over ten years. I wanted to feel passionate about my work, knew I needed help and started working with Kris.*
>
> *My only expectation from the program was that I would see enough improvement by the end of six months so that I felt like I got a good return on this investment. Today was my last call of the six-month program and I would not have guessed that such incredible improvement could be made in such a short period of time.*
>
> *I got unstuck!!! I got my passion back!!! I got the spark again that was suppressed for a long time!! Working with Kris provided me with an unbiased and trained professional who created the space to focus on my goals.*
>
> *It really helped that she never told me what I should do and allowed me to find the conclusions myself within a professional framework. I always felt in control and that I had the ability to find the answers within myself. This was very empowering. I've begun working on my goals for next year. The best thing is that I'm very excited to get started on this next phase and achieve even more in the next six months. Thank you, Kris!!"*
>
> \- Christi Cano, Consultant

"Kris is amazingly organized and thorough. She accomplishes objectives with compassion and sensitivity. She is amazing in her ability to connect closely with people from all walks of life. I recommend Kris highly…she has the gift of encouragement and being able to help people find and reach their calling."

\- Adel Thalos, Associate Pastor, Presbyterian Church of the Redeemer

"Kris' coaching program has helped me examine the things in my life that are important in order to realign my actions to be more consistent with conscientiously maintaining a values-centered life. This program has provided me with a framework to hold myself accountable for living my best life possible and given me an opportunity to regularly prioritize what is important to me so I can align my actions to achieve my personal and professional goals."

\- Alicia Segars, Restaurant Owner

"I was not getting anywhere with my writing and struggling to finish my first novel. After investing in Kris' program, I joined three writing critique groups to better my manuscript. I am also attending conferences and learning how to hone my craft. I am no longer afraid to ask for guidance. I learned that I am worth having the confidence and esteem necessary, and that with a little hard work and soul searching, I can do what I set my mind to do."

\- Cindy Pope, Author

"I am a true believer that people come into our lives for a reason. Kris has allowed me to look at my life personally and professionally and prioritize what is important to me. Her expertise, kindness and compassion are a recipe for success, and I would like to officially recommend Kris if you are interested in becoming CEO of your own life!"

\- Amy Conmy, Sales Manager

"For a long time I put off the notion of hiring an Executive Coach, even though there are many books and professionals that swear by it. When I decided to hire Kris, it was an easy decision. She is one of the most positive people I know and from initial strategy discussions to coaching calls; she had questions and solutions that were completely out-of-the-box. I

admire how she can take a problem and break it down to a process. Process is something I am excellent at in business, but she has helped me see how I can apply it to my personal life as well."

- Todd Nielsen, CEO, Decision Systems Plus, Inc.

"I worked with Kris for only 2 sessions. She was able to quickly sort through my muddled thought process and pin point the main issue I had difficulty identifying, she then helped me to set a schedule that was practical and would help me to achieve my goals. I also read her book "Stuck to CEO" and did the exercises. They were extremely helpful in gaining insight and overcoming the negative thoughts that get in the way of success. I highly recommend Kris if you are seeking a coach to help get you from where you are to where you want to be!"

- Audrey Filardi, Owner, Full Circle Wellness LLC

"I hired Kris for a Strategy Meeting to help me transition more effectively from an employee role into a business owner role. During that meeting Kris helped me gain more clarity around the challenges I was facing and guided me in creating tangible solutions to step out more powerfully in my work and life. By the time the meeting was done I felt more confident about how to proceed and much more certain that I could create the long-term success I desired."

- Larry Megugorac, Owner, Source Point Associates

"I have had the opportunity to work with Kris over the past few months and I am thrilled to note the progress I have made both professionally and personally. I am part owner in a family business and I have had many challenges to work through (as any business owner). Kris has helped me become more proactive in all my challenges and has taught me

tools to become a more effective and productive business person! I highly recommend Kris and look forward to continued relationship with her."

- Jill DelValle, Vice President, Lincoln Family Group

"Kris is an amazing wonder. She has really transformed my life, allowing me to shift what was a high revving engine stuck at 75 in 3rd gear, to a much more manageable 80 in 6th. Much like this example, Kris brings efficiency to each aspect of inner engines. She balances all pieces and allows things to move with greater fluidity – adding lubrication to stuck areas and fuel to already firing synapses. She does it all with an aplomb and professional, yet friendly and fun-loving demeanor. Her work in helping me align my goals, needs, wants and more has been monumental already – and I expect will continue to grow, expand and evolve. Thank you, Kris! I encourage anyone reading this recommendation to act now – not wait 2 years like I did – and hire Kris."

- Andy Greider, Owner of Marketing Pedagogy

"I would recommend that all people speak with Kris for advice on how to juggle their personal lives with their business's needs. It is hard to strike a balance between the two and Kris can show you how to do that as well as many other things to help you realize that life is for living, not existing!"

- Melissa Jennings, Commercial Lines Producer, Stevenson, Shockley, Stevenson, Inc.

Developing A Jabez Lifestyle

Another Shift program you may be interested in is this one:

DEVELOPING A JABEZ LIFESTYLE
Partnering with God to Receive Your Inheritance
A VIP Day Program for Individuals and Groups

If you are like most people, you have every intention of prioritizing the important people in your life, carving out regular time to spend with the Lord, stewarding the resources He gave you for Kingdom impact, and accomplishing the personal/professional goals you are passionate about, along with a strong desire to live out the purpose the Lord has for you. BUT, life, work, and challenging situations seem to keep interfering with your intentions.

You may even be in a season of extreme difficulty where you are questioning the Lord's goodness and wondering why He isn't answering your prayers about the promises He gave you long ago (I've been there, so I completely get it!).

Regardless of what season you are in, the Lord truly desires to bless you and enlarge your territory just like Jabez (1 Chron 4:9-10) so you can receive the inheritance He always planned for you to have (Habakkkuk 2:3) - even if it doesn't feel like it right now within your current circumstances.

If you are thinking, "I don't even know what my Territory is, never mind enlarging it," or wondering, "What does my inheritance even look like?" Then this VIP Day program will be a wonderful opportunity for you to clarify and claim the Territory and promises the Lord has for you.

This program can also be altered for a group to journey through over a weekend retreat or during a one-day event with a virtual preparation call beforehand.

To watch a video testimony from a satisfied client and learn more about the program, go to:

www.BeginToShift.com/vip-jabez-lifestyle

Resources Section

Bible Acronyms Used In This Book:
- CJB = Complete Jewish Bible
- NIV = New International Version
- ESV = English Standard Version

Celebrate Recovery (www.CelebrateRecovery.com)
Their weekly meetings and their 12-step study was truly a transformational experience in helping me process the deep wounds I've experienced from others over the course of my life. They have groups all over the US. So even if you are mildly curious, attend a weekly meeting to check it out in your area. (I also belong to Broken Chains, their motorcycle rider division - I've been riding since 2001).

Restoring The Foundations (a world-wide inner healing ministry): www.RestoringTheFoundations.org

Holy Spirit Documentaries by Darren Wilson Films: www.WPFilm.com

Exploring the Prophetic Podcast on i-Tunes with Shawn Boltz:
 https://itunes.apple.com/us/podcast/exploring-the-prophetic-with-shawn-bolz/id1315785245?mt=2

Prophetic Training
- Graham Cooke: https://BrilliantPerspectives.com
- Shawn Boltz: https://BolzMinistries.com
- James W. Goll: https://GodEncounters.com
- Kris Vallotton: https://KrisVallotton.com

<u>NOTES:</u>

174

<u>NOTES:</u>

Legal Disclaimer

The author and publisher of this book and the accompanying materials have used their best efforts in preparing this book. The information contained in this book is strictly for educational purposes. Therefore, if you wish to apply ideas contained in this book, you are taking full responsibility for your actions.

Your level of success in attaining the results claimed in our materials depends upon the time you devote to the program, ideas and techniques mentioned, your finances, knowledge and various skills. Since these factors differ according to individuals, we cannot guarantee your success. Nor are we responsible for any of your actions. Many factors will be important in determining your actual results and no guarantees are made that you will achieve results similar to ours or anybody else's. In fact, no guarantees are made that you will achieve any results from our ideas and techniques in our material.

The author and publisher disclaim any warranties (express or implied), merchantability, or fitness for any particular purpose. The author and publisher shall in no event be held liable to any party for any direct, indirect, punitive, special, incidental or other consequential damages arising directly or indirectly from any use of this material, which is provided "as is", and without warranties.

The author and publisher do not warrant the performance, effectiveness or applicability of any sites listed or linked to in this report. All links are for informational purposes only and are not warranted for content, accuracy or any other implied or explicit purpose.